# KNOW THY MAN

LEARN WHAT YOUR MAN IS THINKING
**SIMPLIFIED EDITION**

**MANUEL V. JOHNSON**

**KNOW THY MAN – SIMPLIFIED EDITION**
Copyright © 2025 by Manuel Johnson

All rights reserved. No part of this book may be reproduced or transmitted in any form or by any means, electronic or mechanical, including photocopying, recording, or by any information storage and retrieval system, without written permission from the author, except for the inclusion of brief quotations in a review.

Published by: Manuel V. Johnson | Ask Dr Linq, LLC.
Ask Dr. Linq Book Collection

**ISBN: 979-8-9938638-0-1**

Printed in United States of America November 2025
www.AskDrLinq.com

For permissions requests, contact: AskDrLinqInfo@gmail.com

The information provided in this book, *"Know Thy Man,"* is for general informational and educational purposes only. The content is based on the author's research, experiences, and opinions, and is not intended to be a substitute for professional medical advice, diagnosis, or treatment.

Readers should not disregard or delay seeking medical advice because of any information contained in this book. Always seek the guidance of your physician or other qualified health professionals with any questions you may have regarding your health or medical condition. The author and publisher of *"Know Thy Man"* are not responsible for any adverse effects or consequences resulting from the use of any suggestions, products, or procedures described in this book.

By reading this book, you acknowledge and agree that you are solely responsible for your health and wellbeing, and that the author and publisher cannot be held liable for any loss or damage resulting from your reliance on the information presented herein.

# TABLE OF CONTENTS

THE GENESIS .................................................................. 10

JASMINE ........................................................................ 15
    The Beginning ............................................................ 17
    The Greatest Trick ...................................................... 18
    Negativity Is Queen .................................................... 20
    Why Did He Change .................................................. 23
    Waste Of Our Time .................................................... 25

LAUREN ......................................................................... 29
    Watering The Seed .................................................... 31
    The Trophy Effect ...................................................... 34
    The Social Exchange ................................................. 35

ANGIE ............................................................................. 39
    Stuck In Paradise ....................................................... 43
    Dealing With His Baby Mama .................................... 46

NINA ............................................................................... 53
    True Progression ....................................................... 57
    Confuse Her Out of Marriage ..................................... 59
    Man's Fear of Marriage .............................................. 60
    The Haystack Paradigm ............................................. 62
    The Mental Wife ......................................................... 64
    Who's Paying for Our Love ........................................ 66
    Change for Better or Worse ....................................... 68

- She's Every Woman .................................................................. 69
- Break the Curse ........................................................................ 71
- To Sum It All Up ....................................................................... 73

NYANI ............................................................................................. 75
- Our Words ................................................................................. 78
- Programmed To Be Silent ...................................................... 79
- Ask The Right Action Questions .......................................... 81
- Aggressive Responses ............................................................ 82
- The Quiet World of Texting .................................................. 84
- I'll Deal with It Later ................................................................ 85
- Speak Up .................................................................................... 86
- Final Words .............................................................................. 87

TIARA .............................................................................................. 89
- Programmed To Cheat ............................................................ 93
- Lust For New Women ............................................................. 96
- Why Men Sleep With Less Attractive Women ................. 98
- Sex Is Treated As An Award ................................................ 100
- Doesn't Know Worth ............................................................. 102
- She's Familiar .......................................................................... 104
- The Great Male Sexual Ego .................................................. 105
- Before He's Ready To Settle Down .................................... 107

LEXI ............................................................................................... 111
- Why Did You Miss The Red Flags ...................................... 114
- Bad Men Selection ................................................................. 118
- Reevaluating Your Standards ............................................. 119

Why Live a Lie ..................................................................121
What Version of Him Do I Pull Out .....................................122
He Refuses To Get a Legitimate Job .................................124
Is There Love After Heartbreak .........................................126

COURTNEY.............................................................................129
Love Gained And Lust Lost ...............................................131
His Sex Drive Has Declined ..............................................133
Relationship Has Lost Its Passion .....................................136
He Doesn't Compliment Me Anymore ..............................138

NESSA.....................................................................................143
Maternal Protagonism........................................................146
Addicted To Fixing Men.....................................................149
Failing With A Loser ..........................................................152
Who Is the Alpha Female...................................................154
The Bread Winners............................................................158
Financially Insecure Men...................................................161

BRANDY .................................................................................165
The Sad Man .....................................................................168
His Low Self-Esteem..........................................................171
Negative Energy.................................................................172
Healing His Anxiety............................................................175
The Lost Man.....................................................................177

ASHLEY..................................................................................179
Control Freak ....................................................................182
Breaking Her Confidence ..................................................183

- The Financial Cage .......... 185
- Love Drought .......... 186
- Hands On .......... 187
- She Likes Bad Boys .......... 189
- Ego Is God .......... 190
- Safe Exit .......... 192
- Post-Traumatic Awareness .......... 193

ARIANA .......... 197
- The Nonchalant Guy .......... 202
- Big Dick Energy .......... 204
- Emotionally Unavailable .......... 206
- You're the Prize? .......... 216

HALLE .......... 219
- Children in a Bad Environment .......... 222
- Boundaries Between Parents .......... 224
- Incoming Incarceration .......... 226
- Prison Promises .......... 228
- Death of a Parent .......... 230

AVA .......... 233
- He Doesn't Find Me Sexy Anymore .......... 237
- He Had Sex With My Best Friend .......... 239
- He Says He Still Wants Me... He's Lying .......... 241
- His Friends Are Now Hitting On Me .......... 243
- The Gossip King .......... 245

LESLIE .......... 249

- The Can and Want Theory ............................................. 252
- Listen to Her Body ...................................................... 254
- Emotional Intimacy ..................................................... 256
- Unmet Physical Desires ............................................... 258
- Downtown .................................................................. 260
- Anti-Toy ...................................................................... 263
- Sexual Intelligence ..................................................... 264
- Managing Body Insecurities in Intimate Moments ....... 266
- The Guilt Trip .............................................................. 268

SARAH .............................................................................. 271
- The Stepfather ............................................................ 276
- The 2nd Dad ............................................................... 277
- Dads Not Around ........................................................ 278
- If It Wasn't For Your Mother ........................................ 280
- Listen To Your Child .................................................... 282
- The Biological Father .................................................. 284
- Fathers ........................................................................ 287

MARY ................................................................................ 291
- My Dearest .................................................................. 296
- Life After Death For Her .............................................. 298
- How Does He Feel ...................................................... 301
- Life's Last Stop ........................................................... 305

# THE GENESIS

Welcome to a real and honest journey into the world of relationships. What you're reading was created from years of conversations, experiences, and hard-learned lessons. Some readers will find closure from old pain. Some will gain new hope for what's ahead. And many will walk away with a deeper understanding of how love, communication, and truth really connect. Just like art speaks differently to every person, these words will speak to each heart in their own way.

For those familiar with the Ask Dr. Linq platform, the mission has always been clear - to bring understanding and compassion to women who want to know how men truly think. This work continues that same mission, but with more depth, more honesty, and more transparency than ever before. This Simplified Edition was created to make every message easier to take in - without losing the heart or meaning of the original. It speaks directly, clearly, and with the same intention: to bring truth, healing, and understanding to women everywhere.

Everything shared here comes from real stories, real people, and lessons that come from experience, not theory. They were shaped through countless conversations with women who reached out through messages, emails, and phone calls, searching for clarity and peace of mind. They were also shaped by men from every background - married, single, spiritual, nonreligious, successful, struggling, and everything in between. Across all those stories lies one truth: an understanding shared among men that many women have never had the chance to hear.

These insights open doors to awareness, growth, and healing for anyone willing to read. The goal is simple - to help each person connect the dots between what they feel, what they see, and what they've been through. To offer peace where there's confusion, and perspective where there's pain. May these words help heal what's been broken, inspire conversation, and create space for growth and reflection.

Thank you for reading, and thank you for taking this journey through *Know Thy Man*.

# KNOW THY MAN

# THE BOOK OF
# JASMINE

WHERE HAS HE GONE

In the comfort of her bed, phone in hand, Jasmine contemplates whether the guy she gave her number to is genuinely interested. In those initial weeks, he epitomized the perfect gentleman, regular calls, swift responses to texts, and thoughtfully planned dates. Now, with her head against a plush pillow and limbs intertwined in her sheets, she eagerly awaits his response.

Reflecting on the cherished moments they've shared, Jasmine ponders the potential she once saw in him, now reduced to a distant memory. *"Am I overreacting?"* she asked herself. Striving to rationalize his recent behavior, she contemplates the possibility that his demanding work schedule might be to blame. As the sunsets and darkness blankets the sky, worry begins to gnaw at her. *"Maybe I moved too fast. Was it just a forgetful night for him?"* she wonders, a drop of regret coloring her thoughts.

After a couple of days, he finally decides to text her back. A simple "Hello stranger" appears on her screen. With an internal smile but a facial expression that hints at disbelief, she ponders on Kayden's return. It's not the first time he's gone off the grid for days. All Jasmine desires now is an understanding of why these sporadic disappearing acts have become a consistent pattern in their seemingly promising connection.

## THE BEGINNING

When you start dating someone new, always look for the qualities you'd want in a husband. Even if marriage isn't your focus right now, it's smart to pay attention early. Why? Because in the beginning, everything feels exciting and fresh - what's called the infatuation stage. During this time, you might not notice certain flaws because the good moments and the butterflies make everything feel perfect.

You might also be so focused on being the *right woman* for him that you overlook what he's showing you. You're watching how he dresses, what kind of job he has, and how charming he is - all things that can easily distract you from his actual character. His mindset and how he treats people are far more important than what he owns.

At first, you might not be thinking about whether he's husband material, but later, that'll be the only thing that matters. Because once the excitement fades, all that's left is who he really is. When the newness wears off, and his achievements or looks become routine, you'll start to see his true character.

If you notice that he drinks too much, ask yourself honestly - would you want to live with that long-term? Small habits now can become big problems later. The same goes for how he spends his time. If he's always out with his friends and rarely prioritizes you, can you handle that forever?

It's not about expecting perfection or demanding change. It's about being real with yourself before emotions take over. Don't wait until you're in love to start praying that he changes into the man you want. Address what you see now, while you're still thinking clearly.

When you date, remember this: you're not just learning who he is today - you're learning who he might become tomorrow. If you look at him and think, "I could build with that," then you're in a healthy place. But if deep down you know he's not built for your future, don't ignore it.

## **THE GREATEST TRICK**

When it comes to relationships, some men use what I call The Greatest Trick. It's not always intentional, but it's powerful. Here's how it works: he gives you love but tells you he doesn't want a relationship. Those mixed messages keep you hooked - emotionally invested but never secure.

Many women avoid asking, *"What are we?"* because they're scared of pushing him away. But silence is exactly what allows this trick to work. Without clear communication, you're left hoping that things will naturally move toward commitment. Meanwhile, he's enjoying all the benefits of a relationship without the responsibility of one.

In the beginning, he's in the "Make her love me" phase - calling, texting, spending time, saying all the right things. But once he knows you love him, that drive slows down. Now he's in the "I already have her" phase. That's when you start accepting less effort, fewer calls, and weaker commitment - convincing yourself, "He doesn't want a relationship, but maybe one day he'll change."

Here's the truth: most men can handle casual arrangements better than women can. If you agree to something like friends with benefits, ask yourself - can you really separate emotions from the physical connection? If not, it's better to walk away early than to stay and get attached.

And if you're waiting for a man who says he's "not ready," that's your choice - but waiting can become its own trap. His actions might look like love, but his words are telling you otherwise. When that happens, treat him as a friend. Don't give relationship benefits to a man who's only offering friendship.

When you're getting to know someone, make your intentions clear from the start. Ask questions that reveal his mindset. What kind of future does he see for himself? What qualities does he value in a partner? The key is balance - give as much as he's giving, not more.

I remember a woman named Megan who once joked with a guy she wasn't officially dating. She asked, *"Are you cheating on me?"* and he got defensive - acting like she had a right to be upset, even though they weren't together. That reaction showed he felt a sense of ownership but didn't want the responsibility that came with it.

If Megan had asked the right question - like, "Are you seeing other people?" - she could've saved herself confusion. Sometimes you need to ask tough questions to get honest answers. If he says he's single, believe him and treat him accordingly. If he admits he's not exclusive, that's your cue to decide whether you want to stay or go.

Here's something to think about: if a man truly sees a future with you, he'll protect that connection. But if he's okay with a "no strings attached" setup, that's usually all he wants.

So, the next time you're unsure where you stand, throw the bait - suggest something casual and see what he says. The man who's serious about you will refuse it. The one who's not will take it and prove exactly who he is.

## NEGATIVITY IS QUEEN

When it comes to understanding a man's intentions, there are two things to pay attention to - his words and his actions. They should always match. If they don't, believe the negative one.
If he says, *"I want to see you,"* and then never shows up, believe the action.

If he tells you, *"You're the only one,"* but disappears for days, believe the silence.

Men know this - actions speak louder than words - and some use that to confuse you. They'll act like your man, but say they don't want a relationship. They'll do boyfriend things while keeping a single man's mindset. That's how they keep you around.

A man can treat you special even when he doesn't plan to commit. Why? Because he knows you have options. He knows if he stops putting in effort, someone else will grab your attention. So he does just enough to keep you close - just enough to keep you hopeful.

You might think, "If he's acting like he cares, maybe he'll change." But when his actions and his words don't match, that's not confusion - that's control. He's controlling the pace, the tone, and how long you stay.

Sometimes you'll ask yourself, "Why does he want me around if he doesn't want a relationship?" The answer is usually simple: sex. Most men don't get sex as easily as women think. Even men who seem to have plenty of options often don't get the women they actually want. So when they find someone who gives them what they desire - physically, emotionally, or even just through attention - they hold on.

**Here's the rule:**

- When his actions are an A+ but his words are a D−, believe his words.
- When his words are an A+ but his actions are a D−, believe his actions.

They both have to line up. Otherwise, you're setting yourself up for confusion and disappointment.

### IN COMMITMENT, ACTIONS RULE

Once you're in a committed relationship, his words matter less than his behavior. If he says, *"I love you,"* but constantly disrespects you, love isn't what he's giving - it's what he's saying. You need to feel it more than you hear it.

If he says something hurtful like, *"I don't love you anymore,"* don't just react - study his tone. Was it said in anger or sadness? Was it a real confession or an emotional outburst? His actions afterward will tell the truth. But **don't ignore** the words completely - sometimes, words reveal the direction his heart is leaning before his actions follow.

### WHEN DATING, WORDS RULE

When you're just dating - not exclusive, no titles - his words matter more. There's no contract, no commitment, no vows. It's all talk until proven otherwise. You're still in the campaign stage, like a politician asking for your vote. He's telling you what he will do once you give him a chance. Pay attention to what he's saying because that's all you have to go on until he earns your trust.

But once you give that vote - once you make it official - actions take over. You're no longer judging the promise; you're judging the performance.

So remember this: whether you're dating or already committed, the two must always align. If his words and actions don't match, it's time to walk away.

## WHY DID HE CHANGE

After a while, you may notice a man start to act distant. There are a few reasons this can happen. Sometimes, he got what he wanted - sex, attention, validation - and now that need is filled, he's ready to move on. Other times, he confused his own emotions. He might have truly believed he liked you, but once he got close, he realized it was desire, not love.

Men often mix up lust with genuine interest. It's not always about lying or playing games - sometimes he really thought he wanted you until the excitement faded. Once the mystery is gone, he realizes the connection wasn't as deep as he imagined.

There's also the chance that he saw something in you that made him step back. Maybe it was an attitude, a habit, or just an energy that didn't sit right with him. That doesn't mean there's something wrong with you - it just means you weren't his match. Everyone isn't meant for everyone.

People change for different reasons, and not all of them are bad. The key is recognizing where you stand while the shift is happening. Are you both still moving in the same direction, or are you trying to hold onto something that's already slowing down?

If his energy starts to fade, your job isn't to chase it. Your job is to pay attention. If the same effort and consistency that brought you together start to disappear, you have every right to address it. Hold him accountable for the standards he set in the beginning.

Every new relationship carries risk - there's no guarantee of forever. That's why boundaries and respect are crucial early on. When he crosses one, don't ignore it. Tell him directly. You can't expect him to respect limits that you don't enforce.

A man's reaction to your boundaries will tell you a lot about him. If he pushes back, complains, or calls you "too much," he's showing you that he's not ready for a grown-woman relationship. But if he listens and adjusts, he's showing you that he respects your value and his role in your life.

A man will always treat you based on what you allow. If you let him test your boundaries without consequence, he'll keep doing it until there's nothing left to test. Never trade your self-respect for your feelings. You can love him deeply and still say, *"That's not okay."*

Because in the end, your emotions are temporary, but your dignity lasts forever.

## WASTE OF OUR TIME

Have you ever had a man chase you hard for your number - calling you beautiful, flattering you, saying all the right things - only for him to disappear right after you give it to him? Maybe you got a few *"good morning"* texts, and then silence. You start asking yourself, "Why did he even ask for my number if he wasn't going to use it?"

Here's the truth: a lot of men are wired to chase. For them, the excitement isn't in having you - it's in getting you. The chase feeds their ego. It's a small win, a mental trophy that says, "I can still pull her." Once they've proven that to themselves, many lose interest and move on to the next challenge.

Now, not every man who pursues you has bad intentions. Some just lose steam when the effort stops feeling rewarding. Others might be caught in a cycle of chasing attention because it's tied to how they define masculinity.

For them, the pursuit is a form of validation.

But here's what's changed over time - the modern man has evolved alongside the modern woman. A lot of men have experienced being used for free meals, free drinks, or free entertainment. They've dealt with women who had no real interest beyond the benefits. Because of that, many men now look for balance. They want to feel that the energy they give is being matched.

If he senses that you're not as invested, he'll fall back. The modern man doesn't want to feel like he's auditioning for your attention while you keep your options open. He wants effort - not just access.

That said, some men lose motivation simply because they've been chasing for too long. After running in circles, collecting numbers, and building short-lived connections, the thrill wears off. What started as a game becomes routine. They chase for the rush, not the result - and once they realize that, they quietly disappear.

At the end of the day, your peace is worth more than someone's half-effort. Protect your time and your energy like currency. If a man's effort doesn't add value to your life, don't be afraid to cut it off.

You don't owe anyone your energy just because they asked for your number. Guard your space and save your attention for people who actually know what to do with it.

## Read Jasmine's story again - what do you think she should do?

# THE BOOK OF
# LAUREN

**I THINK HE'S THE ONE, BUT AM I THE ONLY ONE**

Lauren, with a heart of excitement, believed that the turbulent times were finally behind them. The initial phase of their relationship had been rocky, as many are. There were moments when doubt lingered, questioning Caleb's intentions, suspecting him of seeking only physical intimacy. Yet, in the dance of time, Caleb proved himself to be more. He patiently waited for three months before their relationship blossomed in a physical one, eventually showing Lauren an erotic side of him she hadn't anticipated. Fast forward five months, Lauren found herself immersed in Caleb's world. She had met his mother, his child, and a circle of his closest friends. Expressions of love flowed freely between them, weaving a web of shared dreams and aspirations. Though residing in separate homes for now, discussions about eventually moving in together had filled their nights. Lying in bed after a delightful evening, they playfully explored the hypothetical details of a future wedding, discussing colors, bridesmaids, and groomsmen. The trajectory of their relationship seemed positively set.

However, nestled in the cocoon of contentment, a seed of doubt sprouted in Lauren's mind. A fleeting curiosity led her to explore Caleb's social media presence. As she delved deeper, she realized that, to the external world, he might appear to be a solitary figure living a seemingly single life. The initial warmth began to cool as doubt slithered through her thoughts like a snake in a dry field of grass. An unsettling realization tightened her stomach - the possibility that Caleb might be keeping their relationship a secret from the world. Despite the undeniable bond they shared in private, the nagging question lingered: *"Am I a secret?"* The uncertainty cast a shadow over the once bright landscape of their relationship, leaving Lauren in a contemplative state, grappling with the duality that now clouded her perception of their love.

# WATERING THE SEED

This phrase describes what happens when a man meets a woman who decides to wait before having sex. Picture it like planting a seed in the ground - he plants it, waters it, and waits for it to grow into a tree that produces fruit. But while that tree is still growing, he's not starving. He's eating from the other trees he planted before.

He doesn't stop enjoying those other fruits just because a new one is growing. He just spends more time watering the new tree - showing attention, calling, texting, bringing food, acting thoughtful - until it's ready to "bear fruit." In this situation, you are the seed, the friendship is the soil, and his attention is the water. When he finally "picks the fruit," that's the moment sex happens.

Here's the main point - a man will wait for sex if he can still have sex elsewhere. Some men water several seeds at once, and whichever one grows fastest is the one they pick first. This is especially true for men who have too much free time and not enough focus in their lives.

Waiting three months doesn't automatically mean he's abstaining. You might be the only one waiting - he isn't. But that doesn't mean you should stop making a man wait; it just means you should know what's really going on.

Some men will lose interest when they realize sex isn't coming soon - and that's actually good. It weeds out the ones who were never serious. His texts will slow down, and his energy will fade. That's how you know he wasn't invested beyond the physical.

Younger men, especially those in their 20s, might wait longer because they usually have multiple women they're talking to. So waiting for you isn't hard - you're just one more seed in the soil.

Men in their 30s and 40s are usually less patient. They're busier, they've played the game for years, and now they want results faster. They might even say things like, "I'm too grown to be playing games," without realizing that they're the ones still playing. Unless you both clearly agreed that it's a casual "sex-uation," his rush toward sex is a red flag.

You can't avoid the watering process altogether - but you can manage how it's done. Steer conversations toward the mind, not the body. Talk about life, beliefs, goals - real things. Texting all day won't help you truly learn who he is. Talk on the phone. Meet in person. Make him use his mouth to speak, not just to kiss.

Nowadays, a lot of men text just to check in and keep the door open for later - so they can come over and "check in" another way. Don't let that be your story. Talk about mental things, not just physical ones. See where his head is, not just his hands.

And remember - just because he's waiting for sex doesn't mean he's waiting for sex. If you're curious, ask a simple question: "Are you sleeping with anyone right now?"

If he says no and you find out later that he was, then you know what you're dealing with. If he says yes, then you decide whether you want to share him. Either way, you've set a standard - you've shown him that who he sleeps with matters to you.

From there, he either has to...
1) Run his game carefully.
2) Be honest.
3) Leave because he realizes things just got real.

Men should practice saying no to sex before they ever get into a relationship. It teaches discipline. Relying on a relationship to stop you from cheating is weak - you must learn to stop yourself first.

If a man has never said *"no"* to temptation, how will he do it when he finally has someone he loves? Women have more practice saying no because they get approached more often. Men don't get that same training - so when the moment comes, they often fail the test.

A man who can turn down temptation shows strength. He's mastered control, not just desire. And that kind of discipline?

That's real masculinity.

## **THE TROPHY EFFECT**

A lot of women believe that meeting a man's parents automatically means he's serious about them - but that's not always true. Some men introduce a woman to their mom simply because she's beautiful, not because they're planning a future with her. If she happens to be at a family event, he might say, *"Hey, this is my mom,"* just to show her off.

Meeting his mother might seem meaningful, but sometimes it's just him showing that he's proud to be seen with you. It's not about love or long-term plans - it's about presentation. The same thing applies when you meet his kids. For some men, introducing you to their child is casual. Maybe they grew up meeting their mom's boyfriends, so to them, it's not a big deal.

The same goes for his friends. A lot of men introduce new women to their crew not because it's serious, but because it's part of their routine. They love to show off a pretty face - to them, that's the "trophy effect." You become proof of their ability to attract beautiful women.

Yes, meeting the people close to him can be a good sign. But it doesn't always mean you're special - it just means you're next in line. What really matters is not who you've met outside of him, but who he is inside. You can meet his mom, his friends, his child - but still not know him.

Think about it - most of those people you can find on his social media anyway. So what has he really revealed to you that wasn't already public? Meeting them shouldn't be mistaken for meeting his true self.

Don't mistake being shown off for being valued. A trophy looks great on a shelf, but it doesn't mean it's cherished - it's just displayed.

## THE SOCIAL EXCHANGE

A lot of men use the "privacy" excuse when they don't want to post their woman online. You've probably heard it: "I'm just a private person. I don't want everybody in my business." But let's be real - if he's still posting about his new shoes, his car, his gym selfies, and his food, he's not private; he's selective. He's choosing what to keep private, and that's usually you.

If privacy were really his concern, he'd delete his social media altogether. But since he hasn't, you have to ask - what's he really protecting? Because when we love something, we don't hide it. We show it. If he's proud of his new sneakers, why can't he be proud of the woman beside him?

Most times, the truth is simple: he doesn't want to mess up his chances with other women. Even if he's not actively seeing anyone else, he doesn't want to close that door. Some women don't care if a man is taken, but posting you might make things harder for him with the ones who do. So instead of being honest, he hides you under the label of "privacy."

Sometimes he'll say things like, *"My child's mother is crazy,"* or *"I do music - it'll ruin my image."* Maybe it's *"My family is nosy,"* or *"Social media isn't real life."* But the bottom line is always the same - he's protecting his freedom, not your feelings.

If you've already met his friends and family, and he's excited to show you off in person, then clearly he's not hiding you from them. So who's he hiding you from? Probably the other women he's entertaining or hoping to entertain later.

A man who truly values you won't let his fear of losing options outweigh your need to feel secure. A relationship is supposed to be mutual - if he cares more about other women's feelings than yours, then that says a lot about where you stand.

Now, this isn't to say that posting you online equals love or loyalty. But refusing to acknowledge you publicly - especially while sharing everything else - is a red flag. It's not about seeking attention; it's about accountability.

If he can proudly show his car, his food, and his new haircut, he should be able to show the woman who's holding him down. And if he claims that social media "doesn't matter," then tell him to let you manage his page for a week - let's see if it still doesn't matter.

Love shouldn't need to be hidden to survive. And a man who's truly proud of his woman will never make her feel like a secret.

## Read Lauren's story again, what do you think she should do?

# THE BOOK OF
# ANGIE

## WHY CAN'T I LET HIM GO

Angie and Mike have been dating for five years now. They have a beautiful two-year-old child together. But it hasn't been the loving ride they had expected.

In the very beginning of their relationship, Angie questioned Mike about having kids. He denied having any children. A year into their relationship she receives an inbox online. It was from a woman she had never met before. The woman on the other end informed Angie that she too had been dating the same guy and in fact she was pregnant by Mike. Angie was highly upset and couldn't believe what she was reading. She asked Mike about the woman and his alleged child; she even let him see the message. His response ultimately was, *"She's lying."* Angie loved her man and as time went on, the situation dwindled away, and she forced herself to believe him.

Eleven months later when Angie was visiting her family out of town, she received a concerned phone call from Mike's mother who sounded bothered with something. She confessed that her son had another child from another woman and stressed that he wasn't in the child's life how she wanted him to be. His mother felt that Mike's lack of attention to this newfound child was due to Angie being around and she didn't approve of this secrecy. Angie didn't want to believe it, but she couldn't just sweep it under the rug this time. She came back home to address the issue face to face. After hours of, *"Why are you tripping?"* questions, he finally admitted that he had slept with someone else, but he claimed it was just once. He stressed that the baby was more than likely not his because it was a one-time situation. She wanted answers, so she encouraged him to take a DNA test. He did, the baby turned out to be his. Angie was upset but more importantly cut deep by the shattered glass of her trust. She later found out that this woman was in fact someone he knew from middle school.

Angie and Mike split and moved into separate apartments; she couldn't deal with the pain she felt every time she saw his face. Angie loved her man unconditionally. So, after months of slowly communicating with one another, they became a couple again. *"He has a baby, we have a baby,"* became her motto. She was very supportive of the situation even though she was somewhat hurt. She eventually developed a cordial relationship with the other child's mother as well.

They continued to stay in separate places and that concerned Angie, but they proceeded to see one another.

In time Angie also became pregnant with his child. She was excited and felt even more connected to the man she so deeply loved. But their separate living conditions continued to concern her regarding his faithfulness. She asked him if he was still sleeping with his other child's mother, and he assured her that he wasn't. She trusted him, but not enough to keep her from his phone. One day she went through it and found some alarming pictures and messages. Messages from a woman she has never seen. When questioned, Mike gave her the same rhetoric he normally does.

They split again but, in a few months, they were back as if nothing happened.

Some time passed and she found out he still was having sex with his child's mother as well. Mike wasn't a new man at all, he simply hasn't changed. At this point, Angie was tired of the cycle she seems to be trapped in. She just wants to get out and into a situation that is more productive to a positive life. But for some reason she can't seem to break away from his grasps. Even though she can see he is not what she needs, he continues to be the one she wants.

## **STUCK IN PARADISE**

The reason you may feel like you can't let him go is because of hope, faith, and belief. Deep down, you still think there's a chance you two can make it work. That's understandable, because most relationships have good moments mixed in with the bad. Those good moments usually stand out more - like nights when he gives you a massage while you watch a movie together. When you've had a **hundred** of those moments and only a few bad ones, it feels impossible to leave. The numbers make it look like the relationship is worth saving - but that's *Quantity* talking.

*Quality* talking says, "Sleeping with your sister might only be **one** bad time out of a hundred good ones, but that **one** bad time hits harder than all the good ones combined." So remember, *Quality over Quantity*.

There's also comfort in someone you've invested time in. You don't want to start over with somebody new. But that's part of the problem - you're looking at it wrong. Don't think of it as starting over with another person. Think of it as improving your life with a new beginning - for you. When you walk out of your house, you're not thinking about running back inside; you're thinking about what you're about to do next. The same mindset applies to leaving a relationship. The opposite of being in a relationship isn't being with someone new - it's being single. Single means one. You.

You may also feel stuck because you haven't reached the point where you need it to be over. You just want it to be over. There's a difference. You haven't gotten mad enough or hurt enough to override the love you still have for him. Once your peace of mind matters more than your feelings, you'll find the strength to walk away.

Sex plays a part, too. When the sex is great - or worse, the best you've ever had - letting go feels harder. It can even create fear. Fear that no one else will ever make you feel that way again. Fear that you'll live the rest of your life unsatisfied. Sex is one of the most powerful experiences two people share - it's intimate, emotional, and spiritual. Breaking that bond isn't easy. The only way to win that battle is to master your own desire. Practice self-control. Take a break from sex and from porn. Yes, that means tucking that rose deep into your drawer.

Another reason you may feel stuck is because you want to win. You want to be the woman who changes him, who makes him better, who he finally chooses. You may not see it that way, but it's a quiet competition inside you. If he picks you, it makes you feel like you're the better woman. Even if the "prize" isn't worth much, it still feels like a prize. Winning him feeds your ego and makes you feel validated - even if what you won isn't gold.

You might consciously want to leave, but subconsciously, you don't. The goal is to build new habits and a lifestyle that don't include him, so that your victory isn't getting him back - it's growing past him. You must replace thoughts of him with a goal in life.

Find something big to focus on - something that benefits you or your child. It could be working out and getting in shape, going back to school, or starting a small business. The point is to pour all the time and energy you used to give him into something that improves your life. Don't try to erase love - redirect it. Let him be replaced by purpose.

You must view him as the *enemy*.

Not as a terrible person, but as an obstacle standing in your way. Picture him as someone trying to block your progress, someone trying to keep you from moving on. He's not your peace; he's the wall between you and it. Seeing him this way makes saying "no" easier. This trick works for breaking any habit. I once quit smoking cigars by pretending the craving was a little evil spirit trying to trap me. Every time I wanted one, I laughed and said, "Nope, you're not getting me." Sounds silly, but it worked. Once you can see your temptation for what it is, you can fight it - because now it has a face.

You have to establish a new relationship with him - one that only involves the child.

If you share a child, keep your communication strictly about the child. Stay polite, stay short, and stay focused. Don't drift into old conversations or jokes about the past. That's how emotional doors reopen. Until you both are mentally detached, there's no need to act like best friends. When you talk, keep it about your child - how they're doing, what they need, or how each of you are doing mentally. Too many people mistake missing someone for wanting them back. Constantly reminiscing about "the good old days" can trap you in an illusion. Those days don't exist anymore - they're memories. Don't build your future on flashbacks.

If you don't share a child with him, remove all contact.

Unfollow him. Block him if you need to. Delete his number and text threads. Move your pictures of him off your phone - put them on a flash drive if you can't delete them completely, but don't keep them where you can see them. We connect with people through our senses - sight, sound, and touch. If you stop feeding those senses, your desire for him weakens. Memories may linger, but they'll fade with time.
Where your attention goes, your energy flows. Focus it on your healing.

## DEALING WITH HIS BABY MAMA

This topic can get complicated because every situation is different. Still, there are a few common patterns worth paying attention to.

## DEALING WITH A BABY MOTHER THAT CAME BEFORE YOU

This is the most common scenario - and usually the easiest to accept.

As you get older, you'll notice most men already have children. The average man becomes a father around twenty-five, which means once you're dating men in their late twenties or thirties, finding one without kids becomes rare.

Pay close attention to how he talks about and interacts with his child's mother. No matter what he says about her now, he once chose to have a child with her. That decision tells you something about him. If he speaks with respect, that says a lot. If he constantly bad-mouths her, that says even more.

When they can't communicate or get along, it automatically puts you in a stressful position. If they barely talk, it can make things look peaceful for you at first - no communication means no drama - but silence can also show immaturity. Ask yourself: does he have a "forget it" attitude, or is he trying to improve the situation for his child? Those answers will reveal the type of man he is.

If he and the child's mother aren't speaking, you might not have to deal with her directly. But if he's trying to rebuild communication for the sake of his child, you can help bridge that gap with his approval. Sometimes the two parents are both hurt and stubborn, and the child ends up caught in the middle. If you stay calm and respectful, you can actually help them build a civil co-parenting relationship - and that gives you some peace too.

Still, it's not your responsibility to fix their issues. You can simply let them handle it themselves. But if you care about him, helping him keep things peaceful can reduce everyone's stress - especially the child's.

Now, what if things between them seem a little too friendly? Like when he says he's at her house playing with his son and somehow "falls asleep" on her couch and doesn't answer your calls? That's when boundaries come in.

When you're in a relationship, both sides deserve respect. He needs to make sure his loyalty is clear. His connection to her should only involve their child - not personal conversations, not late-night talks, and definitely not emotional support. She shouldn't feel like she still has access to the man she used to have. He needs to set that line - not you. She should respect your place, and he should demand that respect. She's connected to him through the child; you're connected to him through love.

Many women wonder if their man is still sleeping with his child's mother. It happens, but not always. Most of the time, he's not - mainly because she doesn't want to. She's moved on and doesn't want to be used again.

Other times, he avoids it because he knows she can't keep secrets. She might tell everyone - including you. So even if he wants to, fear of getting caught keeps him away.

But when she hasn't moved on, jealousy can drive her to stir things up. She might see your happiness with him as proof that she failed. To get her control back, she may tempt him with sex. And if he still craves attention, it's easy for him to give in. In her mind, sleeping with him again means, *"He may be with you, but he still wants me."* But the truth is, he just wanted sex - not her.

Sometimes, she just misses his body, not his heart. She doesn't love him - she loves the way he makes her feel. And his ego feeds off that. It makes him feel wanted and powerful. That's how many men end up caught in the same loop.

### DEALING WITH A BABY MOTHER THAT CAME DURING YOUR TIME WITH HIM.

This is when he got another woman pregnant while still in a relationship with you. That's one of the biggest betrayals a woman can face.

The simple answer for most women is: you don't deal with it. And that's perfectly okay. Leaving is not a weakness, it's self-respect.

But some women choose to stay. And while I understand why - love, time, family - it's a path filled with pain.

## If you stay, there's a lot you'll have to accept.

***First***, you must accept the cheating itself.
***Second***, you have to accept that he likely had unprotected sex with her. Even if he claimed the condom broke, he made a conscious choice to keep going. That means he risked your health.
***Third***, you have to accept the deep level of disrespect that came with it - the carelessness, the lies, the risk of disease, and the possibility of a new life created outside of your relationship.

And ***lastly***, you'll have to deal with the child and the child's mother - for the rest of your relationship. Even if you avoid her personally, she's now tied to your life.

If you truly choose to forgive and rebuild, he has to earn that forgiveness. Boundaries must be clear. He and the other woman must have limited contact - only about the child. They've already shown they can't be trusted with unguarded communication.

Some couples manage this by having the two women communicate directly about the child, turning it into a partnership for the child's sake - not a friendship. But even then, the trust between you and him will always need repair. You'll have to ask yourself: can you ever trust him again?

## DEALING WITH A BABY MOTHER THAT CAME DURING YOUR BREAKUP AND RECONNECTION

While this is rare, but it happens. He got someone pregnant while you two were apart, then came back wanting to start fresh.

It's painful because even though you weren't together, it still feels like betrayal. You might tell yourself it shouldn't matter - but it does.

Breaks often fool people into thinking time apart will fix the problems. But unless those problems are faced and solved, they'll still be there when you come back together.

A "break" also gives him space to live out the temptations he's been fighting. Whether that's other women or just more freedom, he gets to explore it. But when he returns, he may come back with baggage - like a new child.

If this baby was conceived right after your breakup, it raises questions. Was he really single when it happened? Or was he already sleeping with her before? And if it was someone new, what does that say about his judgment?

Check the timing. If the math doesn't add up - if you were only apart for two months but the baby's due in six - something's off.

If you still decide to stay, know that forgiveness must come with structure. You're not just taking him back; you're taking on everything that comes with him - including his new child. You can't say yes to one and no to the other.

Sometimes it's too much. And that's okay. Some women choose peace over pain. You agreed to one life and were handed another.

You have to ask yourself one question: are you rebuilding something that's already broken beyond repair, or are you just afraid to start over?

## Read Angie's story again. What do you think she should do?

# THE BOOK OF
# NINA

**WILL WE EVER PROGRESS & GET MARRIED**

Nina sat on the edge of her bed in the suffocating darkness, absentmindedly twirling her Promise Ring around her finger. Her mind was a whirlwind of thoughts and doubts, wondering where her relationship with Darin was headed. After eight long years together, what once felt like an exciting journey now seemed to have come to a standstill. She had always dreamed of marrying the man she loved and having children. While part of that dream had come true - she had a child from a previous relationship. She found love with Darin, but the finishing part of her dream seemed out of reach. Nina had made her desire to be married clear countless times, but Darin never seemed to share her enthusiasm. The Promise Ring he gave her many years ago, now worn and dull, was a symbol from a time of pain and forgiveness. Looking back, she realized that the ring had been a *Get out of the Doghouse-FREE* card for Darin; a way for him to buy more time, a tool to delay the inevitable conversations about marriage.

Three years after accepting his *"promise"* ring, Nina stopped bringing up the topic of marriage altogether. She had decided to *go with the flow*, suppressing her own desires in the hope that things would eventually change. But deep down, the question never left her mind. *"Will we ever progress?"* a pang of sadness echoing through her heart.

Every night, as she lay next to Darin in the dark, she couldn't help but feel a growing sense of unease. The silence between them felt heavier with each passing day. She remembered the joy and excitement of their early days together, the plans they made, and the dreams they shared. Now, those dreams felt like distant memories, overshadowed by the stagnation that had crept into their lives. Nina glanced at the clock, its neon glow piercing the darkness, marking the late hour.

She sighed deeply, feeling the weight of the years pressing down on her. Her child, now older and more perceptive, had started to ask questions too. *"When are you and Darin getting married?"* they'd ask innocently, eyes full of curiosity. Nina never had a good answer.

She stood up slowly, walking to the window and looking out into the quiet night. The world outside seemed so still, yet within her, a storm raged on. She wondered if Darin even realized how much this unresolved issue hurt her. Did he see the sadness in her eyes? Did he feel the distance growing between them?

The Promise Ring, once a symbol of hope and commitment, now felt like a shackle. It reminded her of unfulfilled promises and lingering doubts. She twisted it around her finger one last time before slipping it off and placing it on the nightstand. She couldn't help but feel a tear escape down her cheek, a silent testament to her internal struggle. Nina knew she couldn't go on like this forever. She needed answers, clarity, and above all, she needed to know if there was still a future for them. With a heavy heart, she resolved to have the difficult conversation with Darin. It was time to face the reality of their situation, no matter how painful it might be. The question of whether they would ever progress could no longer be ignored, and Nina was determined to find out the truth, for her sake and for her child's.

## **TRUE PROGRESSION**

Many people misunderstand the real purpose of being in a relationship. It's not just about being together - it's about growing together. But what does "growing in love" actually mean? Too often, we focus more on the big gestures or ceremonies of love instead of the real meaning behind it.

Before you sign a marriage license or spend half your savings on a wedding, make sure the two of you are growing as individuals and as a team. There's a difference between growth of your relationship and growth in your relationship. Both are good, but they aren't the same.

Growth *"of"* your relationship is the natural timeline most people follow - meeting, dating, falling in love, getting serious, marrying, and maybe having kids. That order might change, but the formula stays the same. It's what we were raised to believe in, and it's often tied to religion or tradition.

A lot of people chase this formula believing that once they reach the end, happiness will follow. They ignore all the warning signs along the way, thinking marriage or children will magically fix everything. But the truth is, marriage isn't the goal - growth is. Marriage should be the result of two people already growing in love. The ceremony is simply a public promise to continue that growth together.

Unfortunately, many couples break that promise because their relationship never had a foundation of real growth to begin with. They chased the idea of being in love instead of living out that love. Like my mentor once said, *"A car with no brakes might move fast, but it's the slow, steady drive that lets you enjoy the view."*

Growth *"in"* your relationship means both of you are evolving as people because of each other. Maybe he encourages you to get healthy. Maybe you motivate him to start that business he's been dreaming about. You could be teaching him meditation to help with stress, or he's teaching you new ways to manage money. Together, you're making each other better.

That's what true growth looks like. It's not about buying him things he couldn't afford before. It's about sharing knowledge that helps both of you elevate. Ask yourself - what value do you bring to his life? How are you helping him improve as a man? What gifts are you sharing that make his world better?

When we say "become one," that's what it really means - combining your strengths, talents, and knowledge to create something greater. If he raps and you sing, make a song together. If you both love creating, build something meaningful as a team. Even your children are the perfect example of this - they're a combination of your best traits.

True progression is growing through your relationship - not just inside of it. This kind of growth has no limit; it lasts forever. It's about always learning, always building, and always evolving together. Marriage, then, is the public promise that you'll keep doing that until death.

The growth of your relationship might end with the wedding and kids, but the growth in your relationship never ends - because in life, if you're not growing, you're slowly dying.

## Confuse Her Out of Marriage

Some men, often without realizing it, use subtle tactics to keep a woman unsure about marriage. I call this "confusing her out of marriage." It's similar to The Greatest Trick - the goal is to make her love him enough to stay, but uncertain enough to stop asking for more.

He may start by planting small doubts in your mind. You might hear things like, "We can't even get along now, imagine being married." It sounds harmless, but it builds fear. Before long, the idea of marriage starts to feel risky, even dangerous. It's not that you don't want it anymore - it's that he's made you afraid of it.

This fear is psychological. Our instincts are wired to run from what feels unsafe. So if he attaches negativity to the idea of marriage, your body will react as if it's protecting you from harm. You'll start telling yourself reasons why marriage isn't a good idea, thinking those reasons are your own.

Here's what's really happening: he knows you. He knows your limits. He knows how to calm you down, and how to keep you around. So what does he do? He gives you just enough love to make you stay, but enough confusion to make you stop pushing forward.

Sometimes he creates chaos - arguments, financial strain, or emotional distance - so you'll feel the relationship isn't "ready" for marriage. Other times, he creates comfort. He'll give you everything a marriage offers except the title, making you feel like there's no need to make it official.

Both situations work to his advantage. The first keeps you too stressed to want marriage. The second keeps you too comfortable to care about it. Either way, he gets the same result - your loyalty without the commitment.

He clouds your judgment just enough to keep you in love, but not enough for you to walk down the aisle.

## **Man's Fear of Marriage**

Today, both men and women experience fear when it comes to marriage - but for different reasons. And surprisingly, men's fears often don't stem from love itself, but from what surrounds the idea of marriage.

Many men aren't actually afraid of marriage; they're afraid of the wedding. Standing in front of a crowd, making vows, being the center of attention - these moments trigger a fear of performance, not a fear of commitment. The weight of public promises can feel overwhelming. Hundreds of eyes watching, waiting for him to live up to every word - it's pressure that can make even confident men nervous.

For others, it's not the crowd but the concept. Marriage feels like the "end" of something - the end of freedom, the end of excitement, the end of adventure. But what they fail to see is that marriage is also a beginning. It's not the end of love; it's the start of deeper love.

Still, many men carry the mindset that once they marry, the chase is over. And that's a problem. Because for most women, marriage represents being chosen. It's validation - a sign that she's special enough for a man to stop searching. But for men, it can feel like losing the thrill of the hunt.

Here's the truth: most men don't spend their lives looking for *"the one."* They just meet someone they like, enjoy being around her, fall in love, and keep going. They don't plan their love story - it just happens. But when marriage enters the conversation, they start to question if this is it. *"Am I done searching? Is there someone better out there?"* Those thoughts aren't about you; they're about his maturity.

A man who truly understands growth knows that marriage doesn't end freedom - it deepens it. It gives him a partner to explore life with instead of running through it alone.

And if he says marriage *"won't change anything,"* ask him this: *"If it won't change anything, then why not do it?"*

## THE HAYSTACK PARADIGM

Imagine reaching into a giant haystack filled with money. Inside are countless $1 bills and a few rare $100 bills. Here's the rule: you can keep every $1 bill you pull out. But if you ever pull out a $100 bill, you can only keep it if you stop searching - and you have to drop all the $1 bills you've already collected.

Now, most people would keep grabbing $1 bills, enjoying the quick reward. Some would stop the moment they found a $100 bill, satisfied with what they've earned. Others would get greedy, thinking they might find another one if they just keep digging.

This haystack is a lot like how some men view relationships. The $1 bills represent easy women, short-term flings, and temporary pleasure. The $100 bill represents the one woman who has real value - the wife.

For many men, the thrill of pulling $1 bills feels more exciting than holding onto a $100 bill. The $1 bills are easy, fast, and come with no responsibility. But once a man commits to that $100 bill, the game ends. He's out of the haystack. No more chasing, no more bragging, no more competition.

But here's where ego comes in. When his friends are still in the haystack collecting, laughing, and boasting, he starts missing the game. He remembers the excitement and begins to feel like he gave something up. Some men even drop their $100 bill - losing a woman of true worth - just to go back to the haystack and prove they've still "got it."

This isn't really about sex - it's about identity. The haystack represents the lifestyle he's used to. Marriage, on the other hand, represents maturity. And the fear of losing what's familiar can make a man sabotage what's valuable.

The truth is, growing up isn't about leaving fun behind - it's about learning what fun is worth keeping. The haystack might look exciting, but it's endless, repetitive, and empty. A man who's wise enough to stop searching will find out that holding onto one $100 bill can be more rewarding than chasing a thousand $1 bills.

## **THE MENTAL WIFE**

Every man carries in his mind an image of his "ideal wife." This woman doesn't exist in *real life*. She's a collection of traits, experiences, and fantasies built over time. Since childhood, he's been gathering ideas about what a wife should look like, sound like, and act like. He's learned it from movies, music, family, religion, and the women he's met along the way.

This woman becomes his *Mental Wife.* She's the standard he compares every real woman to, even if he doesn't realize it. The problem is, she's often unrealistic. She's too perfect, too flawless, and no human being can live up to her.

So, when he meets you, he might love you, but part of him is still searching for her. He might say he wants to marry you, but something in him keeps waiting for the woman who fits that mental picture exactly. And until he accepts that this woman doesn't exist, commitment will always feel like settling.

As he grows and experiences new things, his Mental Wife changes too. She adapts to his new world and his new standards. If you grow with him - share his experiences, challenge his thinking, and add value to his life - you might start to match the image of this woman in his mind. But if your paths grow apart, that image drifts further away from you.

That's why some men stay in long relationships without getting married. They love their girlfriend, but in their head, she's not "the one." They're waiting for a feeling or a person that may never come.

Women love to ask, *"Can you see yourself marrying me?"* But I'd say the question is, *"Who have you always seen yourself marrying? What are her qualities and what does she look like?"*

If his response is, *"I never really thought about it,"* that means marriage isn't a current goal of his. But that doesn't mean a *Mental Wife* hasn't been formulated in his subconscious; it may just mean he has yet to tap into it. Or he just wants to avoid describing someone who isn't you.

If he merely answers, *"You, are who I've seen myself marrying"* he could be giving you the answer he believes you want to hear. It sounds sweet, but his actions will eventually tell you if he's sincere. A marriage should be in the works.

The *Mental Wife* isn't always based on love. Sometimes she's based on ego. Sometimes she's a mix of women he's dated - one who cooked, one who listened, one who matched his ambition, one who satisfied him sexually. He takes the best from each and turns them into one imaginary person. So, when he meets you, he compares you to all of them combined.

But love isn't about matching an idea. It's about learning, evolving, and accepting. The woman he thinks he wants may not be the one he truly needs.

True love isn't built in the mind - it's built in real time, through shared experiences, growth, and understanding. That's how a woman becomes unforgettable.

## Who's Paying for Our Love

Money is one of the biggest reasons some men hesitate to get married. Not because of love itself, but because of what comes with it - the cost, the pressure, and the fear of what could happen if things go wrong.

Traditionally, weddings are expensive. Families once covered the cost - her family paid for the ceremony, his family handled the dinner - but that's not the case anymore. Today, most couples pay for it together. They save, plan, and spend thousands of dollars for one day. To many men, that feels like a bad investment.

He may think, *why spend all that money to impress people who won't even be in our lives a year from now?* He'd rather put that same money into something that lasts - like paying off debt, buying property, or investing in a business. And honestly, that logic isn't wrong. But this mindset often causes conflict because, to many women, the wedding isn't about showing off - it's about celebrating love.

The truth is, this isn't really a marriage problem. It's a wedding problem. You don't need a grand event to be married. Courthouse marriages, small private ceremonies, or even destination elopements are all valid. The real commitment happens after the celebration ends.

Still, some men fear marriage for reasons deeper than money. They fear divorce. They've seen other men lose everything - houses, savings, custody, peace of mind - and they don't want to take that chance. Even if they don't have much to lose, the idea of losing anything makes them feel unsafe. It's not always about greed - it's about control and survival.

For men who own businesses or assets, this fear runs even deeper. They start thinking about prenuptial agreements and legal battles before they even think about wedding vows. To a woman, that might sound cold. But to him, it feels like preparation, not rejection. It's his way of protecting himself in a system he doesn't fully trust.

Love should never feel like a business deal, but when paperwork gets involved, it can start to look that way. That's why communication is key. Talk about expectations early - who's paying for what, what marriage means to each of you, and what fears exist on both sides.

Because for love to last, it has to feel safe. And safety comes from trust, not contracts.

## CHANGE FOR BETTER OR WORSE

When a man falls in love, attraction is usually part of the equation. The physical appeal of a woman often plays a major role in the beginning. Her smile, her shape, her energy - those things draw him in. When she enhances those traits, it reignites that spark. But when those same traits begin to fade, his interest can start to fade too. It's not the only reason love weakens, but it's one of them.

Throughout life, men hear jokes and warnings about what happens "after marriage." They hear that women stop trying once they get the ring - that they let themselves go, stop dressing up, or lose their fire. For some men, it's a real fear. They fall in love with the chase, the effort, the energy she showed while trying to win him. When that effort disappears, it can make him feel like she's gone too.

But here's the truth: that mindset isn't fair. It's based on shallow expectations and often on the wrong examples. Marriage isn't supposed to be the finish line - it's supposed to be the start of something deeper. When both partners commit to staying healthy, not just for each other but for themselves, that spark stays alive naturally.

The fear of someone "letting themselves go" can be avoided by making health and self-care a lifestyle, not a temporary goal. It's not just about the gym or diets - it's about showing pride in who you are and continuing to grow as an individual. The same applies to men. A woman shouldn't have to carry the pressure of maintaining physical perfection while her man stops trying altogether.

Love is much bigger than looks. A real man values a woman who takes care of herself, inside and out, because it shows discipline and self-respect. But if he expects her to stay fit and glowing, he should match that energy too. If she's drinking smoothies and hitting the gym, he shouldn't be drinking beer and making excuses.

The goal isn't to stay the same person you were at the start - it's to grow together into healthier, better versions of yourselves. Because you can lose the abs and still keep the attraction. But if you lose respect and effort, that's when love really starts to fade.

## She's Every Woman

As a man moves through life, he meets many different women - each with something unique to offer. One might inspire him, another might comfort him, another might excite him. Over time, without even realizing it, he starts to piece together the "perfect woman" in his mind.

A mix of every woman who ever made him feel something.

Women do this too, in their own way. Every relationship teaches us something new about what we like, what we need, and what we can't handle. But for some men, this becomes more than growth - it becomes a checklist. Instead of evolving through love, they build a fantasy. Each woman becomes a reference point. One cooked the best meals. One had the best sex. One was independent. One rubbed his feet after work. Now, he wants all those traits in one woman, and if she doesn't have them all, he calls it *"settling."*

This is why some men can't commit. They've built an imaginary woman who doesn't exist in real life. Every new woman is measured against fragments of his past lovers. He doesn't love one woman fully because he's still chasing pieces of many.

The problem is, this kind of man isn't falling in love with a person - he's falling in love with potential. He's not seeing you for who you are; he's comparing you to a collage of memories. And when he realizes you don't check every box, he'll either start pulling away or try to change you into what he thinks he wants.

You can't compete with a ghost. You can't be every woman he's ever known. But you can be the one who stands out by being real.

Because when a man finally matures, he realizes that perfection doesn't come from blending people together - it comes from building something new with one person who's genuine.

You can't force him to accept your version of love. But you can make peace with the truth: if he's still chasing the traits of women from his past, he's not ready to appreciate the woman in his present.

## BREAK THE CURSE

There are men in relationships who aren't really ready for them. They might act committed, say the right things, and even play the part of a boyfriend, but deep down, they're not mentally or emotionally present. Some were pressured into relationships they didn't want. Others convinced themselves they were ready just to keep a woman happy. But when a man isn't genuinely ready, the relationship becomes an obligation, not a choice.

Sometimes he blames her for pushing him too hard, saying things like, "You're the one who wanted this," or "I told you I wasn't ready." And maybe he did. But whether he said it or not, he went along with something he didn't believe in, and that's where resentment begins. He starts to feel trapped instead of chosen. A man who feels trapped doesn't think about commitment; he thinks about escape.

For these men, marriage feels like an even bigger trap. If they can't handle accountability in a relationship, they definitely won't handle the weight of vows and forever. And for some, that fear isn't just about the woman - it's about themselves. They know they're inconsistent. They know they're selfish. They know they still crave attention and validation from others. Deep down, they know they aren't built for the level of discipline marriage demands.

A man's view of marriage often mirrors the environment he grew up in. If he was raised without a father or watched his parents' relationship fall apart, he might subconsciously adopt those same patterns. A fatherless boy can grow into a man who mistakes freedom for strength. He looks at his absent father and thinks, "He didn't get married, and he was fine." But what he's missing is that absence doesn't equal peace - it's just avoidance.

Then there's the opposite. Some men who grew up fatherless move in the complete other direction. They become determined to do the opposite of what their father did. They want to be husbands and fathers because they're fueled by anger, not healing. They want to prove they aren't like him, but they're still being guided by him - just in reverse. The problem is that anger can't sustain love. You can't build a stable home while using pain as your foundation.

Until a man heals what shaped him, he'll repeat it.

Whether that means being afraid of marriage, rushing into it, or running from it, his choices will always reflect his past.

Sadly, some men also expect one woman to equal every woman they've ever had. They want her to be freaky, calm, nurturing, driven, submissive, and dominant all at once. But that's not love; that's greed.

Breaking the curse means unlearning those false ideas about manhood and love. It means realizing that marriage and relationships aren't trophies - they're responsibilities.

## To Sum It All Up

Marriage is one of the biggest decisions a man will ever make. For a man who struggles with making decisions in general, this step can feel like a mountain. If he avoids risks, hesitates to commit to opportunities, or constantly chooses the safe route, marriage will likely intimidate him too. It's not always the idea of love that scares him - it's the idea of responsibility and permanence.

As a woman, what you can't do is drag a man to the altar. You can't pressure him into a lifetime decision he hasn't made in his heart. Marriage doesn't fix broken relationships; it only magnifies what's already there. If you two can't resolve issues as a couple, exchanging rings won't change that. A wedding doesn't heal wounds - it just decorates them.

The true goal is to build something that can last without titles or paperwork. When two people know how to grow, communicate, and forgive, the label becomes secondary. That's what separates "being together" from truly being one.

Now that you understand the difference between growth of a relationship and growth in a relationship, you can see why some marriages fall apart. Many couples chase the title instead of the transformation. They want the moment, not the meaning. But without internal growth, love becomes stagnant. And when the love stops evolving, life inside the relationship feels stuck.

If marriage is what you truly want, make sure it's for the right reasons. Don't do it because of time, pressure, or outside expectations. Do it because it aligns with who you are, where you're going, and what you've built together.

Remember, marriage isn't *required* to have love and happiness. But for many, on a surface level, it's a sacred way to publicly say, *"We've found each other, and we choose to keep growing - together."*

## Read Nina's story again. What do you think she should do?

# THE BOOK OF
# NYANI

## WHY DOES HIS COMMUNICATION SUCK

Nyani was enduring a particularly trying week at work. New management had swept in, reshaping everything in her department and she desperately needed someone to confide in. Naturally, she turned to Brandon, her boyfriend, hoping to hear his comforting words. Yet, true to form, he didn't respond promptly to her text - a recurring pattern that had begun to wear on her. She was growing weary of his seeming indifference and lack of verbal support. Before they officially became a couple, Nyani had made it clear to Brandon that transparency and open communication were non-negotiable for her. She believed in addressing issues head-on and didn't want to be left in the dark about his feelings either. Brandon, however, admitted to struggling with being an open book, often dismissing his behavior as simply being "himself". Neglecting simple things, like neglecting to inquire whether she wanted food on his way to her place.

As their relationship progressed, Brandon's disinterest in nurturing their connection became increasingly clear. Nyani hoped that by directly addressing their issues, Brandon would open up about his true feelings and intentions. She offered him chances to voice any doubts or reservations, even suggesting they take a break if needed. Each time, Brandon reassured her with hollow promises and assurances of commitment, despite his actions consistently failing to align with his words.

On that fateful day at work, Nyani waited anxiously for Brandon's response to her text, seeking reassurance amidst the chaos of her job. Hours passed before he finally replied, suggesting they meet up to discuss something that had been on his mind. With a sinking feeling, Nyani anticipated what was to come. Brandon expressed his belief that their relationship had run its course, buried under the weight of his busy life.

Nyani felt a surge of anger and hurt, not just because their relationship was ending, but because she had known deep down that this moment would come. She couldn't help but think how much pain could have been avoided if Brandon had been more forthright earlier. Masking her disappointment with a composed demeanor, Nyani calmly acknowledged his decision, choosing not to dwell on the unspoken words and unfulfilled promises that hung between them.

Picking up her purse, Nyani couldn't resist a parting comment, her voice tinged with a mix of sadness and frustration.

*"Now see, that wasn't so hard, was it?"* she said.

Brandon's gaze fell to the floor, unable to meet hers as Nyani walked away, carrying with her the weight of dashed hopes and the ache of a love unreciprocated. In that moment of departure, she mourned not just the end of a relationship, but the loss of the future she had envisioned with him. Yet amidst the sorrow, Nyani found a quiet resolve to move forward. She was determined to heal from the pain of loving someone who couldn't love her back the way she deserved.

## Our Words

Having healthy communication is the foundation of a healthy relationship. But at the most basic level, as people, we communicate in many ways. Words are how we share our thoughts and feelings. It takes awareness to speak with meaning. Actions can be random or unplanned, but our words carry weight - they reveal who we are and what we think.

Our words are our bond. Like a New Yorker would say, *"Word Is Bond."* The Bible says in John 1:1, *"In the beginning was the Word, and the Word was with God, and the Word was God."* The Law of Attraction teaches us to speak things into existence. So clearly, *words* hold power. The ability to turn thought into sound and transfer it to another person is what allows us to connect and build relationships.

If a person doesn't know how to express what's in their heart or mind, their partner won't truly understand who they are.

*Example:* You may come to a party with me because I asked you, but how do you feel about this party?

Words add layers to relationships that actions alone can't. It's often the lack of meaningful conversation that causes distance between partners - the absence of curiosity and important questions. When your partner doesn't express themselves easily, don't assume you already know how they feel. Ask them. Get their side instead of being satisfied just because they went along with what you wanted. Sometimes we're so happy they followed our lead that we forget to ask if they even wanted to.

Our words give breath to our emotions. They are how our soul speaks. Never be afraid to breathe life into something you care about. And also, know when silence is power - especially when words would only feed negativity.

## PROGRAMMED TO BE SILENT

Men often struggle with expressing emotion because many were taught from a young age to keep things inside. Society conditioned them to believe that showing sadness, fear, or pain makes them weak. When a man reacts emotionally after a breakup, people say he's "acting like a woman." That mindset tells men that expressing pain is unmanly. Over time, that message trains them to stay quiet, even when they're hurting.

This silence doesn't disappear when they enter relationships - it follows them. Many men keep their emotions locked away and their words short. They believe that staying calm and quiet is what men are supposed to do. That "suck it up and be a man" mentality might look strong on the outside, but it creates emotional distance. It's why some women are shocked when a man suddenly leaves - they never knew there was a problem because he never said there was one.

We have to make space for men to speak their truth. A man can be strong and still express fear, doubt, or pain. Real strength is the ability to face emotions without shame.

Now, with the rise of social media, we communicate more but connect less. We have a wider reach but less depth. Real conversations have been replaced with comments, reactions, and short replies. The emotion that once came with face-to-face talk has been lost behind screens. Imagine if every conversation had to happen in person - how different the connection would feel.

Phones, texting, and social media made things easier but cheaper. It's like comparing a microwave meal to one cooked in the oven. Both will fill you up, but only one nourishes the soul.

Because of this, many men depend on their phones to express emotion. Confidence in real, face-to-face conversation is fading. We're seeing fewer men who can express themselves clearly and calmly in person. Instead, they rely on screens to say what they can't say in real life.

When a man gets your number, it's just digits on a screen. He texts, you respond, but there's no real energy behind it. The more you text, the less you connect. Eventually, he fades out - not because he stopped liking you, but because he never formed a true bond in the first place.

He never connected with the woman behind the screen - he only connected with her profile.

## ASK THE RIGHT ACTION QUESTIONS

When you're getting to know a man, pay attention to how much effort he puts into opening up. Notice if you always have to ask, *"So, what about you?"* Some men won't naturally share details about their lives unless they're asked directly.

If you decide to keep dating a man who doesn't express himself easily, make your questions clear and specific. Vague questions lead to vague answers.

For example:
- A general question sounds like, *"Can you see yourself in a relationship with me?"*
- A direct question sounds like, *"What needs to happen before you're ready for a serious relationship with me?"*

The first question usually gets you a smooth but empty answer like, *"Yeah, I can. You're beautiful and I like you."*

The second question forces him to think. It asks for details, not feelings. If he says, "I don't know, I never thought about it," that tells you everything - you're thinking about a future he hasn't even considered.

You have to ask questions that require action, not emotion.

Instead of asking, *"Do you still want this relationship to work? Prove it."* say, *"What are you going to do differently to make this relationship work?"*

That switch changes everything. The second question makes him a*ccountable* and requires a list of <u>current</u> steps. If he doesn't have a real answer, how can he fix what's wrong? A man who doesn't know what to do can't lead a relationship anywhere.

Words create promises, but actions prove them. If he can't describe what change looks like, chances are he won't create that change. Can't drive to a home if you don't know what roads to take.

## AGGRESSIVE RESPONSES

A lot of men avoid simple conversations because they know those talks can easily turn into arguments. If you tend to respond aggressively, he'll hold back what he really feels. It's similar to how teenagers stop talking to their parents because they don't want to be misunderstood or scolded. He'd rather stay quiet than risk being criticized.

**Be conversational, not confrontational.**

When someone opens up to you, don't shoot them down or make them feel foolish for what they said. Think of it like someone stepping on stage for the first time to speak publicly - if the crowd boos, they'll never want to do it again. Communication in relationships works the same way. If you embarrass him for speaking up, he'll stop trying altogether.

There's a difference between being "real" and being "rude." You can be honest without being harsh.

If you ask your man how he feels and he gives you an answer you don't like, don't respond with, *"You need to man up and deal with it."* That doesn't make him stronger - it makes him shut down.

A better response would be, *"I believe in you. I know you can handle this. I wouldn't be with you if I didn't believe that."* Those words strengthen him instead of breaking him down. Then you can work together to solve the problem.

If you can't offer comfort, why would he bring his pain to you?

Speak to the man you want him to become, not the boy you want to correct. When you talk to him like his mother, you bring out his inner child. But when you speak to him like his woman - his peace and his support - you bring out the man.

## THE QUIET WORLD OF TEXTING

These days, most of us spend hours with our heads down, staring at our phones. We aren't talking, we aren't moving, but somehow, we're still "communicating." Texting makes it easy to multitask, but it also weakens how we connect.

We've become more open with strangers online while growing more closed off in real life. The more we text, the less we practice speaking. The more we shorten our messages, the more we shorten our thoughts. Eventually, we stop expressing full emotions and start speaking in fragments.

People meet, exchange numbers, and still only text. Sometimes, the first real words spoken come right before meeting up - *"I think I'm outside your house."* That's how bad it's gotten. We're training ourselves to be worse communicators, one emoji at a time. If communication is the key, then we've locked ourselves out of love's door.

Many men naturally prefer quick conversations. Texting lets them stay in control - they can respond when they want and avoid topics that make them uncomfortable. This habit creates selective expression. They talk when they want, but never when they need to. Over time, it builds emotional distance, and when things get serious, you find yourself with a man who doesn't know how to talk to you.

# I'll Deal With It Later

One of the worst habits in relationships is waiting too long to talk about what's wrong. When you hold things in, small problems turn into big ones. Think of it like cancer - you can't see it growing at first, but by the time you notice, it's often too late. Ignoring emotional issues works the same way.

Many men are natural procrastinators. They avoid tough talks because they don't want to argue or feel uncomfortable. But when they keep postponing communication, resentment builds up. Then one day, everything explodes at once, and you're both overwhelmed by ten problems that could have been solved one by one.

Putting off communication doesn't solve anything; it just pushes the problem down the field. The longer you wait, the harder it becomes to fix. Eventually, you get tired of running after peace that keeps moving further away.

If you're with a man who avoids conversations, help him see what that behavior causes. Don't nag or attack him - show him real examples of how it's affecting you and the relationship. Explain that avoiding problems doesn't protect peace; it just delays the argument.

Change starts with awareness. Once he recognizes that his silence creates distance, he can start working on it.

But be prepared - he'll probably make those changes... when he gets to it.

## Speak Up

Being open and honest is the backbone of a healthy relationship. True connection means having one mind - not thinking the same, but understanding each other clearly. That's why so many people say, "Marry your best friend." A best friend is someone you can confide in, not hide from. Someone you can share your heart with, not hold grudges against.

For women, communication is comfort - it keeps them emotionally connected. For many men, communication is more about purpose. They talk when there's a problem to solve or a point to make. In the beginning, he'll talk a lot because he's trying to win you over. But once he feels secure in the relationship, he might pull back. He doesn't see small talk as necessary anymore, because he feels his actions already show his love.

That doesn't mean he stopped caring. It just means he doesn't always speak unless it feels important to him. What's vital to remember is that what's "important" to him might not always match what's important to you.

So instead of assuming he's shutting down, ask questions that open the door. And when he does talk, listen - really listen. You may be great at expressing yourself, but true communication is a two-way street. It's not just about getting your point across; it's also about giving him space to feel safe sharing his.

When a man feels like you're not just his lover but also his friend, he'll talk to you differently. He'll open up more, share more, and trust more. Friends feed the mind, lovers feed the heart. When you can be both, the relationship becomes deeper, more peaceful, and almost effortless - a rhythm that feels like dancing in sync.

## **FINAL WORDS**

Ask direct questions if you want direct answers. Don't dance around what you really want to know-be clear, be confident, and expect honesty in return. When he answers, accept his words instead of dismissing them. You can disagree, but listen. The goal isn't to win; it's to understand.

Technology has made communication easier but weaker. We talk more, but say less. Messages, emojis, and quick replies have replaced tone, body language, and emotion. That's why it's so important to rebuild real connection - to speak with presence, not just convenience.

It's common for men to struggle with expressing themselves. If he can't always say how he feels, he should at least listen deeply when you do. A good listener is just as valuable as a good speaker. Real communication isn't one-sided - it's a cycle of speaking, hearing, and responding with care.

If you're open about your feelings, make sure you're equally open to his. When he does share, resist the urge to interrupt or judge. Let him know that being vulnerable with you is safe. When two people truly communicate, they move as one. When someone sees you as a best friend, they don't hide things - they share their thoughts, fears, and dreams freely. Friends give mental peace; lovers give physical comfort. But when you can be both, a safe space and a spark - you create something rare and lasting.

It's like a dance where both partners know the rhythm. Each step drawing you closer to true unity.

## Read Nyani's story again, what do you think the problem was?

# THE BOOK OF
# TIARA

**WHY GET INTO A RELATIONSHIP IF YOU'RE GOING TO CHEAT ON ME**

Tiara slammed the door of her apartment's gym, the resounding thud echoing through the empty hallway. Without missing a beat, she jumped onto the treadmill and began her assault on the machine. Her feet pounded against its belt, each step a desperate attempt to channel her raging frustrations into something productive. Working out had always been her sanctuary, her escape in times of emotional turmoil, but this time, the storm inside her was unlike any she had faced before. The man she'd given her all to, had given all his manhood to another woman. At 28, Tiara was experiencing the sting of betrayal for the first time in her life, and the pain was almost unbearable. Tiara and Ronny had been a couple for three years; both with child from a previous relationship. They had been planning to move in together, to blend their lives into a semblance of a family, but now those plans were shattered.

Tiara couldn't understand why he would betray her trust. She had done everything he asked for, and more. She cooked his favorite meals, she made love to him whenever he was in the mood, and she never nagged him. What baffled her most was that she always felt he never matched her efforts in the relationship. If anyone should have cheated, it should have been her, she thought. She saw no reason for him to stray, but he had.

She discovered his infidelity through his text messages. Normally, she respected his privacy, but on this day, a nagging intuition led her to check his phone. What she found were conversations and pictures that made it clear he was involved with another woman. When she confronted him, he tried to deflect, focusing the conversation on her trust issues and even questioning her love for him. *"You must be looking for a reason to end this relationship anyway,"* he had said.

After a lengthy argument, Ronny finally admitted to some of her accusations. He basically took a plea for a lesser charge. She didn't convict him of first-degree cheating; instead, he was guilty of *inappropriate behavior with intent to perform a sexual act, and relationship disrespect*. This earned him some time in the doghouse but not a life sentence without her. She loved him, and after three years together, she had shared more experiences and laughs with him than with her two previous boyfriends combined. She didn't want to lose her soul mate after investing so much into the relationship. So, she forgave him. *"Nobody's perfect,"* she mulled over, convincing herself that this was the right decision.

But Ronny hadn't learned his lesson. A year after this first incident, Tiara discovered he had slept with his daughter's mother, Marie. Despite all the derogatory things he had said about his baby mother, he still went back to lay with her. This time, the betrayal cut even deeper. Tiara felt stabbed in the back, because Ronny knew about the hurtful things she had said about Tiara, and he still allowed Marie to have one up on her.

She couldn't take it anymore. She had seen too many friends live in fear of being cheated on and she wanted no part of that endless paranoia. She decided to end her relationship with Ronny and move on with her life. It was clear he wasn't ready to be faithful, so she let him go.

Two years after their breakup, Ronny contacted Tiara on social media with a simple *"Hi."* She was in a good place in her life, so she responded. A conversation ensued, and they exchanged numbers. Days went by without any further contact, but this new interaction sparked Tiara's curiosity. *"What if things could be different?"* she thought. But then, she took a deep breath and deleted his number from her inbox.

But that didn't stop her mind from wandering. *"Why had he cheated?" "Why can I still see us as a couple?"* Just as these thoughts swirled in her head, her phone buzzed with a message alert.... It was Ronny.

## PROGRAMMED TO CHEAT

Since we were young boys, we've been trained without even realizing it to believe that sleeping with a lot of women makes us more of a man. The message comes from everywhere - TV, movies, music, even the men we look up to. Fast cars, sports, fixing things, taking care of your kids - those are all parts of manhood too, but they don't get celebrated like having women does.

The "cool" guy on TV is always surrounded by women. In a lot of songs, being with multiple women - even someone else's woman - is praised. That kind of messaging shapes how young men think. It becomes a belief that manhood is tied to sex and conquest.

Now, if a man chooses to be single and sleep with whoever he wants, that's his decision. Not everyone is built for relationships or even ready for one. But the problem comes when a man decides to commit while still holding on to that "player" mindset. Before committing, he has to first recognize that this programming exists - and that it still has a grip on him.

A lot of boys grow up around older guys - brothers, cousins, uncles - who pressure them to "be a man" by having sex early and often. Girls and boys both get pressure in different ways, but it's rare for grown women to tell young girls to sleep with everyone. Meanwhile, grown men constantly push young boys to do exactly that. So they grow into men who think sleeping with as many women as possible is the goal.

As he grows, that behavior gets rewarded. He's called a "player," a "ladies' man." The more women he sleeps with, the more respect he gets from his peers. It becomes a twisted scorecard - one that tells him his worth as a man depends on how many women he's been with.

That kind of mindset feeds into cheating. Because once he stops chasing women, deep down, he starts to feel like he's losing part of his manhood. The identity that's been built in him for years starts to fade. For what? For one woman? That's why you'll see some men act like being faithful makes them weak. When they get into relationships, their friends tease them for "settling down" or "getting soft."

But as we get older, that teasing stops - not because men suddenly get mature overnight, but because they start realizing that real manhood has nothing to do with how many women you've had.

Still, the programming doesn't disappear easily. Even grown men struggle to shake that mindset. Ask a man why he cheated, and half the time he can't even give a clear answer. You'll hear, *"I don't know,"* or something that doesn't make sense like, "I was lonely," even though you can barely get time with him. The truth is, he doesn't understand why either -

because his actions are still running off the programming.

So even when he loves you, wants to be with you, and wants a family, he still feels like giving up other women is giving up a piece of who he is. Imagine standing on a foundation that you've believed in since childhood, then having to tear it down to be a faithful partner. If that man doesn't have a new foundation built - one based on purpose, discipline, or real self-worth - he'll cling to that old belief system because it's the only thing that makes him feel like a man.

**Fellas, let me talk to you for a minute.**
If the only thing that makes you a man is sleeping with women, then somewhere along the line, you got lost. Real strength isn't about how many women you can sleep with - it's about how much control you have over yourself.

A man earns respect by giving it. If you're chasing women who don't even respect themselves, that doesn't make you powerful - it makes you careless. Being masculine isn't about how many people you can touch; it's about how much discipline you can hold.

That word, *discipline,* is one a lot of men run from. But a man who can control his urges has a strength that others don't. Anybody can give in to temptation. It takes real maturity to conquer it.

Taking a broken woman and helping her rebuild - that's strength. Tearing her down just to feed your ego - that's weakness. A strong man doesn't destroy what he touches; he builds it.

And again, this isn't to judge single men who choose to sleep around. That's their lane. But don't let that lifestyle be the thing that defines your manhood. Don't let your worth be tied to how many women you've been with. Because when you do, your manhood is for sale - and the price keeps dropping.

If you choose a woman who deserves your respect, give it to her. If you don't, ask yourself what that says about you. Any man can chase. But a real one can control himself.

## **LUST FOR NEW WOMEN**

When it comes to cheating, one of the biggest triggers is the temptation of something new. That sense of newness can mess with a man's logic. As a relationship goes on, people get comfortable. They start taking each other for granted. Everything they need is right in front of them, but something in them starts whispering that something's missing. Instead of looking inward, they start searching outside the relationship for a spark that's really supposed to be built within.

Sometimes people look for outside fixes to inside problems. But that kind of fix never lasts. It's like drinking salt water when you're thirsty - it might feel like relief for a moment, but it'll only leave you emptier later.

For some men, that restlessness shows up in their sex life.

He can have a woman who gives him everything - love, passion, and loyalty - but because she's his, the thrill is gone. The excitement of chasing and conquering fades, and he starts craving that rush again. The problem isn't her; it's the mindset that being a man means always needing something new to prove himself.

A man who ties his value to how many women he's been with is constantly looking for his next "win." That chase becomes an addiction. It doesn't stop just because he loves you - in his mind, love and lust live in two different rooms. That's why some men cheat even when they claim to be in love. To them, love is emotional, but sex is ego.

It's like this - imagine eating steak every day. It's your favorite meal, but after a while, no matter how perfectly it's cooked, you get bored. So he starts craving something different - not because the steak is bad, but because he's tired of seeing the same plate. Now, a wise man figures out how to season that same steak in new ways, keep it interesting, and appreciate its quality. But a foolish man? He'll sneak off to grab a pork chop, thinking he's missing out on something.

That's what happens when a man never learned how to find excitement within what he already has. He's used to chasing what's new, not cherishing what's true.

## WHY MEN SLEEP WITH LESS ATTRACTIVE WOMEN

One of the most common questions women ask after being cheated on is, "Why her?" They look at the other woman and think, She's not even cute. She's not on my level. But here's the truth - when a man cheats, it's rarely about looks. It's about ego, opportunity, and access.

If his goal isn't to build a new relationship but simply to conquer, then her job, her house, her looks, or her status don't matter. He's not choosing her to replace you - he's choosing her to validate himself.

To him, every new woman represents a win. Whether she's a "$100 bill" or a "$5 bill," he'll pick up both just to say he got them. It's not about value - it's about collecting. Some men treat women like trophies, and every encounter becomes another addition to the shelf.

Even if she's what others would call "easy," that's a benefit to him. She doesn't challenge him, doesn't expect more, doesn't make him work for it. That makes her convenient. A woman like that fits perfectly into the life of a man who wants to cheat without much effort. She's flexible to his schedule, doesn't ask questions, and often knows her role.

A lot of women think, My man doesn't have the time to cheat. But it doesn't take much. A quick thirty-minute detour, a "traffic jam" excuse, or a fake trip to the store - that's all he needs. And if the other woman already knows he has someone at home and doesn't care, that makes it even easier. He can sneak in, get what he wants, and go home as if nothing happened.

What makes it worse is that men like this often believe they're too smart to get caught. Their confidence blinds them. Each time they get away with cheating, it boosts that false sense of control until eventually, they get sloppy.

When a man cheats with someone you think is beneath you, it doesn't mean she's special - it usually means she was available. He wasn't searching for an upgrade; he was scratching an itch.

And when you ask, "Why would he risk losing me for someone who can't replace me?" remember - in that moment, he's not thinking about losing you at all. He's not thinking about the future, the risk, or the consequences. He's thinking about right now. That's how cheating works - it's impulsive, selfish, and short-sighted.

Sometimes the type of woman he cheats with says more about him than about her. If he keeps choosing women with no standards, no goals, or no direction, that's a reflection of his level, not yours. When a man doesn't recognize your worth, he'll always settle for less. Then convince himself it's enough.

When a man no longer fears losing you, cheating doesn't feel like a risk - it feels like relief. In his mind, he's not choosing "her over you." He's choosing "him over both of you."

## SEX IS TREATED AS AN AWARD

For most men, sex isn't just pleasure - it's validation. Since childhood, many boys are taught that being desired by women is proof of their worth. So when a woman offers herself to him, he doesn't just see it as sex - he sees it as a reward, an accomplishment, a win.

Women have more options when it comes to sex. A woman can get approached three times in a single day. The average man might go three months without anyone flirting with him. So when a woman shows interest, it feels rare, and rarity feels valuable. That's where the addiction starts.

A man who has ten women chasing him might not value sex as much, but he'll still take every opportunity. Not because he's starved, but because it's available. He wants the credit, not the connection. Sleeping with a woman becomes another notch, another trophy, another story to tell himself when he needs to feel powerful.

Think of it like racing. Every driver wants the big championship wins, but even the small races count toward the total record. The man who sees sex as achievement thinks the same way - every encounter adds to his record, even the meaningless ones. It's not about love or pleasure. It's about the scoreboard.

And when he sleeps with a woman, his brain rewards him for it. The chemical rush - dopamine, testosterone, endorphins - feeds that sense of victory. Over time, it's not the sex he craves; it's the feeling of being chosen. He becomes addicted to the idea that every new woman confirms he still has "it."

That's why even after getting into a relationship, the addiction doesn't always go away. Being committed doesn't give him that same jolt. His girlfriend choosing him doesn't feel like a win anymore - it's familiar. He already "has" her.

And here's where the cycle gets messy. When a woman chooses him after being hurt by another man, he may not even realize that she didn't choose him because he's special. She chose him because the last man broke her. But he'll still take the credit.

Men like this grow up believing that sex is something they receive, not something they give. If more men saw sex as something they give - if they valued their bodies the same way they value a woman's - they'd start protecting their energy instead of wasting it everywhere.

If he stopped thinking of the vagina as a $100 bill and his penis as $1, he'd realize every exchange isn't worth the trade. Because if you keep giving your body to everyone, it stops being a prize.

When a man finally learns that his worth isn't measured by how many women he's had, but by how much discipline he has - that's when he's really grown.

## DOESN'T KNOW WORTH

Most men are taught to value women's bodies more than their own. They treat the vagina like it's a $100 bill and their penis like it's $1. So when they're offered sex, they jump at the trade - because who wouldn't swap a dollar for a hundred? That's the problem. Too many men think of themselves as the lesser value in that exchange.

When a man doesn't know his worth, he'll give himself to anyone. He'll say yes to every offer because losing a dollar doesn't seem like much. But in that mindset, he's missing the point - his body has value too. Every time he sleeps with someone who doesn't deserve him, he lowers his own price.

A man who respects his body won't give it away like a free sample. He'll think twice before letting someone access his energy, time, and presence. Because once he learns his worth, sex stops being about validation - it becomes about connection.

When a man starts viewing sex as something he gives, not something he gets, he'll raise his standards. He'll stop seeing women as rewards and start seeing intimacy as a choice that should benefit both people. That's what real value looks like.

## Rate Her Value

When some men think about women, they subconsciously assign value like they're rating cars or clothes. A woman they've never slept with might seem like a "100," but after being with her for a while, that number starts to drop - not because she's changed, but because the man now feels he's conquered her. To him, the excitement fades once he feels he's "had" her.

But here's the thing: her value hasn't gone down. It's only his immature mindset that makes him believe it has. He's addicted to the thrill of the chase, not the substance of the connection.

Some men even keep mental scorecards. If she's slept with a friend or someone he looks down on, her "value" drops before he even touches her. But if she's tied to someone he doesn't like - maybe an ex of an enemy, or someone off-limits - her value rises, not because of her worth, but because his ego sees it as a win.

This is how twisted the thinking can get. For some, sleeping with a married woman or a woman in a relationship feels like the ultimate victory. To them, it's not about love - it's about power. It's about saying, I took what another man thought was his.

But once a man starts valuing himself and the act of sex the same way he values the woman he's with, that whole mindset shifts. He stops thinking like a collector and starts thinking like a builder.

When a man values his body and his energy, he'll stop giving it away to anyone who asks. He'll say no when he should. Because if every woman is worth his time, then his time isn't worth much. When a man's standards rise, so does his peace.

## SHE'S FAMILIAR

A lot of men who cheat don't do it with strangers-they do it with women they already know. Maybe it's an ex, a friend from the past, or someone who's been in their circle for years. There's comfort in the familiar. He doesn't have to start over, explain himself, or put on a show. She already knows his habits, what makes him laugh, what makes him mad, and how to make him feel good again.

With her, there's no pressure to perform as a boyfriend. No expectations about the future. No emotional demands. Just convenience. That's what makes it dangerous-it's easy.

If she's an ex, her motivation might be different. She might be trying to prove to herself that she can still have him. Or maybe she's out for revenge because he once cheated on her. Either way, if she still wants him, she'll make it easy for him to come back. She'll be extra sexual, extra understanding, and extra available. That's her game.

And if he's weak for that comfort, he'll take the bait.

For him, being with her feels easier than being with you - not because you're doing something wrong, but because you represent responsibility. She represents escape. With you, he feels the weight of expectations. With her, it's just sex and ego.

Experienced cheaters know how to keep that separation. They'll sleep with the familiar woman and walk away. The inexperienced ones? They're the ones who fall into the trap - leaving their relationship for the ex, only to realize nothing's changed. The same problems they had before are still there. The only difference now is that he lost a good woman in the process.

And here's another truth - men with great sex skills cheat more. Why? Because the women they've been with don't want to let go. They hold on, hoping he'll come back. They tell him how good he is, and those compliments feed his ego. That ego boost keeps them around, and he keeps them close because he loves how they make him feel like a god.

When you see a man who can't cut ties with his past, it's often not because he loves those women - it's because he loves what those women do for his ego.

## THE GREAT MALE SEXUAL EGO

Men who are great in bed usually know it - and that knowledge feeds them. Over time, hearing "you're amazing" becomes a drug. Every compliment is another hit of validation. Eventually, it's not about the woman anymore. It's about the performance. The applause. The ego.

Once a man has been told for years that he's good in bed, it shapes how he views sex. Pleasing women becomes a mission. But once he's proven himself to you, the thrill fades. You already know he's good. So now, he wants a new audience. Someone else to test his "skills" on. Someone new to confirm what he already believes about himself.

You may tell him how great he is, but he might dismiss your words. To him, your love makes your praise biased. So he looks for a stranger - a woman with no emotional ties - because her reaction feels "pure." When she moans louder, compliments him more, or can't stop texting afterward, it gives him a high no long-term partner can match.

That's why some men cheat - not out of boredom or lack of love, but out of a need to feel exceptional. They want to prove to themselves they still "got it."

Women often mistake a man's attention to detail in bed as love. Sometimes it is, but often it's pride. He wants to perform well because it feeds his ego. Sex becomes less about connection and more about confirmation. He's not making love - he's proving a point.

Ever met a man who doesn't even care if he finishes, as long as you do? He'll focus on your pleasure because your reaction is the scorecard. That praise fuels him more than the act itself.

Now, in a relationship, this can work in your favor if he channels that ego right. If you consistently affirm his performance, his need for approval stays satisfied at home. But if your enthusiasm fades with time, he may start seeking that validation elsewhere. And that's where the danger begins. Because while you're praising his patience as a father or his focus at work, another woman is praising his stroke. She's the one moaning louder, texting him after, making him feel like a king. And the ego inside him - the one that's addicted to approval - goes where the loudest applause is.

It's unfair to you because you love the whole man, not just what he does in bed. But for him, ego doesn't care about love. Ego only wants to win.

## BEFORE HE'S READY TO SETTLE DOWN

A lot of men are taught from early on that being a "real man" means sleeping with as many women as possible. It starts in their teens and keeps getting reinforced through music, movies, and even their friends. That mindset doesn't just disappear when he gets older - it follows him into relationships and sometimes even into marriage.

A man doesn't just wake up one day and decide to stop chasing women. That takes stages. Real growth happens in layers, not overnight.

**First stage**
He stops chasing new women, but that doesn't mean he's done with them. He just becomes more passive about it. Instead of approaching, he lets women come to him. He's not out hunting anymore, but he's still available if they show interest.

**Second stage**
He starts losing excitement for new sex. He's been there and done that. If it happens, fine. If not, no big deal. He's not trying to sleep with every woman he meets anymore, but he's still open if the situation falls in his lap. He becomes more selective, picking and choosing his moments.

**Third stage**
He's narrowed his circle down to a few regular women - maybe two or three - who've been around for a while. He's no longer chasing new women because that takes effort. Now he rotates the same few women when he wants sex. They're his "standbys." If he happens to get into a relationship during this stage, those same women often become his side pieces.

**Fourth stage**
He's simply tired. Tired of juggling, tired of lying, tired of managing emotions. He doesn't want drama or extra women

anymore. He just wants peace. Sex may not be as thrilling as it once was, but he prefers the calm that comes with having one woman. His sex drive might not be as strong now, but his desire for stability finally outweighs his desire for variety.

The problem is, if a man gets married in the first stage, when his lust is still high, the odds of him cheating are higher too. He still has that chase built into him. His woman might feel loved and sexually fulfilled, but that same drive can lead him back to old habits.

If he gets married in the fourth stage, the odds of cheating drop - but so can the spark. His libido might not be as strong, and sometimes his wife ends up feeling less wanted.

Many women find themselves attached to men who show signs that they aren't ready, yet they stay. And often it's because of three emotional attachments: optimism, sex, and ego.

1. Hope that he'll change because he does other things right, like being a good father or showing glimpses of potential.

2. Fear that she won't find another sexual connection that matches his.

3. Ego - the need to win. Not wanting another woman to "take" what she's invested in.

The problem is, you can't out - love a man's lack of discipline. You can't teach self-control to someone who hasn't decided to grow up yet. Look for the man who already practices restraint. If he can say no to simple temptations - like eating what he shouldn't or spending what he doesn't have - he's more likely to resist cheating. Because a man who can't tell himself no, can't be trusted to tell anyone else no either.

## Read Tiara's story again, what do you think the problem was?

# THE BOOK OF
# LEXI

## WHY IS EVERY RELATIONSHIP A BAD RELATIONSHIP

It was over. Lexi had just ended her two-year relationship. Another guy she thought had potential turned out to be a complete screw-up. Time after time, Lexi found herself in the same heart-wrenching situation. She'd meet a guy who seemed to embody many of her favorite qualities, who also promised commitment and sincerity. They wouldn't just use her for a fling; they'd talk of a future together. Some even seemed more eager for a relationship than she did. But inevitably, it all would fall apart.

Lexi always questioned if there was any love left after each heartbreak. And despite finding new potential partners, each attempt only added to her pain rather than healing her wounded heart like many women in her position, doubt began to creep in. She scrutinized her own thinking and reevaluated her standards, wondering if they were too stringent. Eventually, she concluded that perhaps it wasn't entirely her fault, but rather her choice in men.

Her last relationship was with a guy she had known for over a year. Elijah had always flirted with her, though she never took him seriously because he didn't fit her usual type. Despite his charm and good looks, his lifestyle didn't align with hers. Yet he made her laugh and spoke passionately about his goals and interests. In her eyes, he had potential, so when he finally asked her out, she agreed. They clicked. Fresh from a draining relationship, she eagerly embraced his everyday humor as a source of joy.

Months passed, and they became an official couple. Initially, everything was wonderful. But as time went on, cracks began to appear. Elijah's lifestyle, which she had purposely overlooked before, became a growing concern.

He resisted seeking stable employment, his lies multiplied, and inconsistencies surfaced.

Once again, Lexi found herself in familiar despair: another man she had invested her heart in turned out to be a disappointment. Despite stepping out of her comfort zone, hoping for a different outcome, she faced yet another heart break. Now, Lexi asks herself with a heavy heart, "*Am I the problem?*"

## **Why Did You Miss The Red Flags**

When it comes to relationships, it always takes two people. There isn't a right or wrong side - just two perspectives: yours and his. Sometimes we meet someone we're attracted to, and that attraction makes us want to find more reasons to like them. Once we're drawn in by looks, we start searching for qualities that help us connect.

But in that search, we often overlook what's wrong. We're not looking for reasons not to be with them - we're focused on finding reasons to be with them. Like the Bible says in Matthew 7:7, *"Seek and ye shall find."* When your mind is set on building a bond, it'll find things that help that bond grow - even if it means ignoring the truth.

Think of it like when you buy a certain car and suddenly see it everywhere. It's not that there are more of them - your brain is just locked in on that pattern. When you want something, your brain will look until it finds it. That's how powerful focus can be.

At first, your "attachment radar" is on, so you notice the good things. But your "detachment radar" - the part that warns you about problems - is off. So you miss what could hurt you later. You see the potential but not the red flags. You believe it'll work because you want it to work.

That's called confirmation bias - your mind finds evidence to support what your heart already wants to believe.

Once the relationship is official, you start noticing the flaws. The mission's complete - your brain no longer needs to look for reasons to attach. Now it starts spotting the reasons to detach. That's when all the little things you ignored come to light.

He hasn't changed - you're just seeing what was always there. You begin to notice habits, attitudes, and behaviors that don't sit right. When you bring it up, he says you're being controlling or that you've changed. But what really happened is your eyes opened.

You missed the red flags because attraction blinded your logic. You were excited, hopeful, and focused on what you wanted the relationship to be, not what it actually was.

To avoid this, keep a list - mental or physical - of what you don't want in a partner. Review it early, before the relationship even forms. What behaviors cross your boundaries? What values are non-negotiable? Check for those signs the same way you'd check the ingredients on a label before buying something.

No one's perfect, but effort matters. The person for you won't be flawless, but they'll be aware of their flaws and willing to work on them.

That's the real difference between potential and progress.
And most importantly - love with both your heart and your eyes open.

Human beings naturally seek comfort. We like what feels familiar because it feels safe. That's why we tend to repeat patterns - even when those patterns hurt us. The problem is, what feels familiar isn't always what's good for us.

The first man you truly fell in love with often sets the tone for the ones that follow. You fall for traits that remind you of him - his energy, his charm, his humor - not realizing you're falling for a pattern, not a person. You might even say things like, "I like men who do this," or "I'm attracted to guys who work in that field," without realizing those preferences are built on memories, not compatibility.

I've seen women choose one man over another just because of a title - like preferring a man who's a barber over one who's an electrician - even when both have the same values and stability. The issue isn't the job; it's what the job represents to her. She once dated a man with that title who made her feel good, and now she unconsciously chases that feeling again.

This mindset can be dangerous because it causes you to repeat cycles. You're not choosing new love - you're chasing an old comfort. Even if it ended badly, your mind remembers the high before the fall.

That's why many women end up dating the same kind of man in a different body.

This repetition is especially dangerous for women who've been in toxic or abusive relationships. Some confuse chaos with passion. They believe that yelling, tension, or constant drama means he cares. When a calm, emotionally stable man comes along, he feels boring. But the truth is - peace just feels unfamiliar when you've lived in stormy love.

If you've ever said, *"I just can't feel chemistry with nice guys,"* it might be because your body still associates love with adrenaline and anxiety. You can mistake peace for disinterest. That's not love - that's conditioning.

When choosing your next partner, don't chase what feels familiar; chase what feels healthy. The man you loved at 22 taught you what you liked, but he might've also taught you what to avoid. Learn from both lessons.

If you keep attracting the same type of man, ask yourself: is it the men, or is it the way you interact with them? Sometimes the pattern isn't who you choose, but how you show up. If you approach new love the same way you did before - with the same fears, habits, and expectations - you'll get the same result.

Sometimes to attract better, you have to become better.

## **BAD MEN SELECTION**

Sometimes, the problem isn't that you keep running into bad men - it's that you keep choosing them. Not on purpose, but because the kind of man you're drawn to feels familiar. That familiarity feels like comfort, but it's really just what your body remembers from pain.

You might tell yourself, *"I like strong men,"* but what you're actually attracted to is emotional dominance - the kind that makes you chase his approval. You might think, "He's mysterious," but in truth, he's just inconsistent. You confuse his silence for depth, when it's really avoidance.

We often romanticize the traits that once hurt us because they remind us of what we couldn't fix before. That's how cycles start - chasing closure in someone new, trying to win a battle that ended years ago.

If every man you choose leaves you emotionally drained, it's time to question what part of you believes you can heal through pain. The truth is, you can't fix what's broken in you by falling for what already broke you.

Take a step back and study your own pattern. The next time your heart skips a beat for a man who reminds you of the last one, pause. Ask yourself, *"Is this attraction or repetition?"*

Because sometimes, what feels like chemistry is just history trying to repeat itself.

## REEVALUATING YOUR STANDARDS

There comes a time when you might start questioning whether your standards are too high or too low. Life changes us, and sometimes what once felt reasonable now feels out of reach. But before you start lowering your standards, ask yourself - are they truly unrealistic, or have you just been entertaining the wrong kind of men?

For example, wanting a man who owns two homes when you don't own one yet might not be practical. But lowering your expectations just because no one has met them yet? That's not wisdom - that's frustration. Don't let disappointment disguise itself as logic.

Your standards are shaped by what feels comfortable and familiar - your upbringing, your experiences, your beliefs. If you grew up valuing communication, consistency, or financial stability, those things naturally become your baseline. But comfort can be deceptive. Sometimes we cling to it so tightly that we close the door on growth.

You might feel uneasy dating someone who communicates differently than you do or who lives a lifestyle outside of what you're used to. But discomfort isn't always danger - sometimes it's development. Growth often requires sitting in spaces that challenge your normal.

Still, there's a difference between expanding your standards and abandoning your principles. You can be open-minded without being naive. Be willing to grow into higher love, not shrink yourself to fit into lesser versions of it.

Before lowering your standards, consider widening your circle. You may not be asking for too much - you might just be asking from too small of a pool. The right man may not come in the packaging you expect. He might not have the same job title or background as the men you've dated before, but he could have the values you've been praying for.

If you say you only date men who make a certain amount of money or work in a certain field, ask yourself why. Is it about security? Status? Or control? The man who truly meets your needs might not check your list - he might rewrite it.

Your expectations should also mirror what you bring to the table. You can't expect consistency if you're inconsistent. You can't demand patience if you don't give it. Relationships thrive on reciprocity - not perfection, but effort.

A high-value man wants a woman who challenges him to grow, not one who competes with him or tears him down. So yes, keep your standards - just make sure they grow with you.

And remember: the best way to challenge his masculinity is through your femininity. Correct him with grace, not aggression. Instead of saying, *"You're doing it wrong,"* try, *"Would this be a better way?"* You don't have to shrink to lead. But sometimes the softest voice in the room is the loudest.

## WHY LIVE A LIE

The online dating era has made pretending easier than ever. A man doesn't need to study you in person anymore - your social media already gave him the cheat sheet. He can scroll through your posts, your comments, even the quotes you share, and start mirroring everything you say you want. You said you love Paris? He suddenly does too. You posted about loyalty? He's preaching loyalty in your DMs. You're not being pursued by his truth; you're being pursued by his research.

Sometimes he's not even doing it on purpose. Social media naturally gives him access to the blueprint of your desires. But when he's intentional, that blueprint becomes his weapon. He builds the perfect version of himself - not to become that man, but to play that man long enough to win you over.

Why would he do that? Because he believes if he shows you the real him too soon, you'll never give him a shot. His logic is simple: get her attached first, then reveal who I really am. He bets that by the time you see through the act, you'll already be too emotionally invested to leave.

You'll notice the red flag early if you pay attention to pace. When he moves too fast - saying he loves you within weeks, talking about marriage before learning your middle name - that's not romance, that's manipulation through acceleration. He's trying to secure your attachment before his mask slips.

Once the lie runs its course, two things can happen. You either walk away when you realize he's not the man you fell for, or you stay because you've convinced yourself that the real him "isn't that bad." That's how most toxic bonds survive - not through love, but through attachment that outlasts logic.

In his mind, he's taking a risk that can only benefit him. Without the lie, you'd never have looked twice. With the lie, he at least gets what he wants - your time, your body, your attention. If he loses you, he's back where he started. If he wins you, he's gained access to something he couldn't earn honestly.

That's why living a lie makes sense to him. It's not about love; it's about leverage.

## WHAT VERSION OF HIM DO I PULL OUT

Every woman brings out a different version of a man. Some pull out his peace, some his chaos. Some awaken his ambition, others expose his laziness. The question isn't just *"Who is he?"* - it's also *"Who does he become with me?"*

A man's behavior often shifts depending on the woman he's with because every woman has her own standards, energy, and expectations. One woman might tolerate excuses; another might demand accountability. One might laugh off a lie; another might walk away after the first one. So when you hear that he treated his ex differently, he probably did - not because he's two different people, but because she required something different from him.

Think of it like a job. One company allows phones at work; another doesn't. The employee is the same, but the policies are different. His behavior changes depending on what's expected of him. If the job means enough to him, he'll adjust to keep it. If it doesn't, he won't. Relationships work the same way.

Men adapt to the rules of the environment they're in. If you set a standard and stay consistent, he'll either rise to meet it or remove himself because he can't keep up. If your boundaries are weak or inconsistent, you leave the door open for him to shape-shift based on convenience.

And here's the deeper truth - sometimes the version of him you pull out is a reflection of the version of you he's responding to. Energy mirrors energy. A woman at peace often pulls out a man's calm. A woman in chaos often finds herself in conflict. That doesn't mean his behavior is your fault; it means your energy influences the tone of the connection.

You can't control his actions, but you can control your vibration. Stay grounded in who you are. Be kind, but firm. Be soft, but strong. Give him your best, and if he fumbles that, he has to turn you over - not the other way around.

## HE REFUSES TO GET A LEGITIMATE JOB

There may come a point when you start questioning his drive and ambition. Those are usually qualities you look for before things get serious, but sometimes they slip through the cracks. Maybe he said he was *"working on something,"* and you believed him. Or maybe you saw his potential and thought you could help him reach it. But here's the truth - you can't change a man who doesn't want to change himself.

People tend to stick to the life they know until they're convinced that a better one exists for them. If he's always hustled a certain way, it'll be hard to convince him that a 9-to-5 or a structured business path makes more sense. He might even see it as you trying to control him. The only way to reach him is to show him something that feels both familiar and better - not to lecture him, but to inspire him.

Some men simply don't like structure. They want to wake up when they want, move when they feel like it, and live by their own clock. Ironically, those same men usually lose that freedom the moment they get caught up in something illegal. But that risk doesn't always register until it's too late. Many of these men actually have entrepreneurial instincts - they just need direction. The problem is, until life hits them hard - losing their freedom, their family, or their peace - they rarely slow down long enough to see it.

If you want to help him shift, you'll have to show him what a real plan looks like. Talk to him about what he's passionate about, and help him see how that passion could become legitimate income. Make it visual. Write it down. Show him that what he's chasing now could be turned into something sustainable. Some men don't respond to advice - they respond to vision.

But at the end of the day, effort is everything. If he can't put in effort to build a stable future, that's not leadership - that's laziness dressed as independence. A man who won't prepare for life is a man who's preparing to lose it.

Think of it like this: if he's driving straight toward a brick wall and you warn him, but he keeps going, that's not ignorance - that's pride. And pride destroys more relationships than poverty ever could. A real leader listens. He may not agree with every suggestion, but he values the input. Leadership isn't about control; it's about collaboration.

So if he's refusing to step up, refusing to plan, and refusing to listen, then he's not leading - he's drifting. And love can't thrive under a leader who won't lead.

Some men will need to lose you to finally learn that lesson.

## IS THERE LOVE AFTER HEARTBREAK

Yes. There is always love after heartbreak. But before you look for it in someone else, you have to rebuild it inside yourself. Love, joy, and peace aren't things you find in people - they're things you share with people once you already have them within you.

After heartbreak, your energy drops. You might start listening to sad music, scrolling through old photos, replaying memories, and convincing yourself that what you lost can't be replaced. But that's a lie your pain tells you. The truth is, pain narrows your vision - it makes you see only what's missing, not what's possible. To heal, you have to raise your vibration. You do that by rebuilding your confidence, your focus, and your sense of self.

When you can't find progress in relationships, that's your cue to find progress in yourself. Grow your mind, your body, and your spirit. Go to the gym, pick up a new skill, read a new book, or take a trip somewhere new. Even small steps matter. Every time you achieve something new, you stitch another piece of your heart back together. The same effort you once gave to love someone else, give it to improving yourself.

Channel your pain into purpose.

- Start the business you've been talking about.
- Go back to school, even if it's for one class.
- Redecorate your home, change your scenery, or explore somewhere peaceful.

The point is to shift your focus from what left to what's growing. Every goal you accomplish becomes a reminder that you can rebuild. That you can stand again. That your story isn't over.

Here's the best part - when you truly heal, your energy changes. You glow differently. You attract people who are on your frequency because they feel your peace before they even know your name. That's what real healing does: it makes you magnetic.

Think of love like a glass cup. When your heart gets broken, the cup shatters and the love spills out. You can't pour new love into a broken cup; it will just leak out again. So before you look for someone new to fill you, you have to fix your own cup. You do that by filling yourself with self-love, spiritual peace, and personal growth. Once that cup is full, it naturally overflows - and that overflow is what real love feels like.

When you finally heal, you'll stop seeing heartbreak as an ending and start seeing it as a beginning. You'll realize that what broke you didn't end you - it prepared you.

It built a version of you that can love deeper, see clearer, and walk stronger.

So yes, there is love after heartbreak. But first, there's healing. And once you've found that love within, you'll never beg for it from anyone again.

## Read Lexi's story again, what do you think the problem was?

# THE BOOK OF
# COURTNEY

**OUR RELATIONSHIP HAS LOST ITS FIRE**

The bedroom plunged into darkness the moment Courtney switched off the television. She shifted in bed, shielding her ears from the rhythmic snoring of her boyfriend, another night passing without intimacy. Doubts gnawed at her; was she the root of this disconnect? She thought. Although Malik seemed more open with his emotions, his physical interest in her appeared to dwindle.

After four years of deep love, it was the absence of passion that troubled Courtney most. The once bright spark in his eyes when he looked at her had dimmed to a mere flicker. She had changed her hairstyle three times this month alone, yet he hadn't noticed. Compliments were few, and any sweetness felt obligatory, lacking genuine warmth.

Sex had lost passion, feeling more like a chore than a shared pleasure. Most days, Malik showed no interest in intimacy. Even when they did make love, Courtney kept her shirt on, self-conscious about the slight weight gain around her waist. She began to blame herself, questioning if she was the cause of their diminishing connection. When she brought the subject to Malik, he brushed her concerns aside, dismissing any notion of trouble. In her heart, Courtney feared he might be seeing someone else.

# LOVE GAINED AND LUST LOST

**Love:** An intense feeling of deep affection.

**Lust:** Very intense sexual desire.

When a man first meets a woman, his attraction is usually physical. Her jokes may seem funnier, her energy more exciting, and her flaws easier to overlook. It's not because she's perfect - it's because he's drawn to her appearance. But over time, the physical attraction fades slightly, and what starts to grow stronger is the emotional and mental connection.

It's hard to build emotional intimacy without shared experiences, but the more memories two people create together, the stronger that connection becomes. With time, love begins to outweigh lust. The passion may not burn as hot, but the bond becomes deeper.

When a relationship begins with heavy passion, it usually changes as the excitement cools. In the beginning, he might see her as an exciting partner, full of energy and fire. But as life shifts - she becomes the mother of his kids, his teammate, his peace-the relationship moves from thrill to trust. It becomes more meaningful.

Eventually, he may see her more as a nurturer than just a lover. This stage isn't negative; it often means the bond has matured. It's a sign of growth. But here's where it gets complicated - if he no longer feels lust and doesn't know how to rebuild it with her, he might seek that excitement elsewhere.

That doesn't always mean his love disappeared. His love could still be growing, just not yet at its highest level. True love doesn't allow cheating. So when a man cheats, it's often because his emotional maturity hasn't caught up with his affection. His love hasn't reached the stage where it's strong enough to deny temptation.

Love develops in stages. It grows through effort, respect, and consistency. The highest form of love is when a man wants what's best for you, even if it costs him something. That kind of love is unconditional - it's built, not born overnight.

So while he may love you, his love might not yet be deep enough to stop him from chasing lust elsewhere.

This is why, as emotional closeness deepens, physical passion sometimes fades. For him to fill you with love, he has to pour out the lust that once drove him.

The closer the emotional connection becomes, the more the focus shifts from excitement to intimacy.

Real intimacy isn't just about touch - it's about connection.

- Emotional intimacy: sharing truth and vulnerability.
- Intellectual intimacy: connecting through thoughts, curiosity, and growth.
- Experiential intimacy: bonding through time and shared life moments.

The more you build in these three areas, the stronger the passion becomes - because your hearts are involved, not just your bodies. Balancing love and lust is hard, but essential. Lust fades quickly; love lasts. Lust is the spark. Love is the flame that never stops burning.

Most women can have a man's lust. Few will ever hold his love.

## His Sex Drive Has Declined

There are many reasons a man's desire may fade, and not all are your fault. Men's bodies change as they age. As testosterone lowers, their drive naturally slows.

Some may not feel it much, while others notice the difference and quietly turn to help without saying it.

For most men, testosterone peaks in their 20s, then begins to drop. That hormone controls not only muscle and energy but also passion and drive. When it dips, it's like running low on gas.

Beyond that, mental stress can also affect him. Performance anxiety - when a man worries too much about performing - can block desire completely. When stress hormones rise, they restrict blood flow, and that kills confidence. If this happens, it can be frustrating for both of you, but especially for him.

It's not always physical. Sometimes it's mental or emotional. He might feel embarrassed or worry that you'll judge him. Many men hide it, pretending everything's fine. But healing starts with honesty. If you're gentle and open, he may eventually share what he's going through.

Sometimes, it's not a health issue at all - it's distraction. He may be using other outlets to manage his desire, like self-pleasure or fantasy. This doesn't always mean he's doing something wrong, but it can leave his partner feeling left out.

It raises questions like: *"Is he thinking of me or someone else?"* *"Has he lost interest"*

Some men use those outlets as a way to release tension and avoid making bad choices. Others might fall deeper into it until it hurts their intimacy.

If his drive has dropped because of another woman, that's a different conversation entirely. But don't assume that's always the case. Sometimes his body or mind just isn't in the same place it used to be.

Ways to help him rebuild energy naturally:
- Drink more water
- Eat balanced meals high in protein
- Exercise often
- Sleep more
- Reduce stress
- Avoid masturbation

His confidence and desire can come back. But it takes patience, peace, and partnership - not pressure.

## **RELATIONSHIP HAS LOST ITS PASSION**

Many women struggle to keep the spark alive in their relationship. Intimacy is more than just physical closeness - it's the deep emotional connection that makes you feel safe, understood, and wanted. It's that bond that says, we're in this together, even when life gets hard.

At first, intimacy often shows through touch - you can't keep your hands off each other, you're excited just to be near them. But true intimacy is tested when sex isn't an option. When there's still affection, laughter, and attention in those moments, that's when you know the bond runs deep.

When passion fades, it's rarely just about the bedroom. It's about emotional distance - the small cracks that form when communication weakens, when routines take over, or when trust gets shaken. Sex might still happen, but it starts to feel like repetition instead of connection.

Familiarity can be dangerous. When two people get too comfortable, they start to assume each other will always be there. The effort fades. The compliments fade. And soon, it feels like the passion has gone missing.

But passion doesn't die - it just needs oxygen again.

**A FEW FACTORS THAT CAN HELP PROMOTE PASSION AGAIN ARE:**

• Resolve any trust issues that may have shaken your mutual trust. It's very difficult to look at your partner with passion if you are aware of lies they've told you.

• Spend time outside the house together. A change of scenery can help break the cycle of repetitive, robotic routines.

• Hold hands more often. Studies show that holding hands releases oxytocin, promoting bonding and a sense of togetherness crucial for intimacy.

• Give each other massages. Caressing your partner stirs up emotional responses and demonstrates care and compassion for their physical well-being.

• Share non-relationship - related fears. Intimate conversations about personal fears can lay the groundwork for physical intimacy through emotional understanding and empathy.

- Kiss different parts of the body unexpectedly. While a kiss on the lips is common, unexpected kisses on the forehead, chest, or inner forearm can evoke different emotions and invite intimacy.

- Begin sexual encounters from a different position each time. Starting sexual routines differently and keeping them fresh helps maintain excitement and break the monotony.

- Have sex in different places around the house. Changing locations, like the kitchen or living room, can bring a new level of excitement and create memorable experiences distinct from the bedroom.

Once trust is rebuilt, routines are refreshed, and both hearts are open again, passion returns naturally. Love just needs space to breathe.

## HE DOESN'T COMPLIMENT ME ANYMORE

It's a painful feeling when the person who once couldn't stop praising you suddenly goes silent. When someone we love stops noticing us the way they used to, it can shake our confidence. You start asking yourself questions: *"Did I change? Did he? Am I not attractive anymore?"*

But here's the truth - sometimes, it's not about you. People have a habit of losing interest in the things they once cherished. It happens with possessions, hobbies, and yes, even relationships. When the thrill of something new wears off, it reveals how genuine the connection really was.

Physical attraction is usually what catches his attention first. That initial spark can be intense, but it's surface level. It's easy to be mesmerized by beauty and chemistry. What's harder - and what lasts - is building attraction through emotional connection and respect. That's what transforms infatuation into genuine love.

If his attraction was only skin-deep, it may fade when the excitement does. But when a man truly grows to love his woman, he finds beauty in her natural self - her laugh, her quirks, even her imperfections. When the love is real, he doesn't stop seeing you; he sees more of you.

Now, that doesn't mean you should reinvent yourself just to regain his attention. Your worth isn't tied to how often someone compliments you. If he loved you through your best days, he should still love you through your changes. Real love adapts - it doesn't vanish when your hairstyle or body does.

If his compliments have slowed, talk about it. Be open. Don't demand praise, but express how acknowledgment helps you feel seen. Healthy love thrives in communication, not assumption.

Compliments aren't just about flattery - they're reminders that we're appreciated. When you stop hearing them, it can make you feel invisible. But remember: their silence doesn't erase your value.

No one wants to feel taken for granted, especially by the person they love. A few words of affirmation can reignite connection and reassure both partners that the relationship still matters.

Love is built on effort, not perfection. If someone leaves because your body changed or your look evolved, that says more about the shallowness of their love than about you. True love grows roots - it doesn't float on the surface of attraction.

So keep giving him reasons to be proud to have you by his side. Keep shining, keep improving, and know that even if his compliments fade, your light shouldn't. Because when a woman knows her own worth, she doesn't need to be reminded - but she'll never settle for someone who forgets it.

# Read Courtney's story again, what do you think she should do?

# THE BOOK OF NESSA

**ARE YOU GOING TO PAY FOR THIS**

He slammed the front door in Nessa's face, and she refused to open it again. Their last words had been as venomous as the bite of an African black mamba, a fitting end to the worst argument they'd ever had. After these verbal clashes, Joseph always fled to his mother's house to unburden himself, ignoring Nessa's pleas for them to resolve their issue within their own home. To her fiancé, this never seemed to be an option.

Nessa thrived in her high-paying job at an advertising agency, while Joseph barely managed to make ends meet on his own. Despite their financial disparity, money had never been the foundation of their love. For Nessa, it wasn't about material possessions but about the emotional support that couldn't be bought - a kiss on the forehead and a listening ear were worth more than any new handbag.

Initially, their differing financial situations seemed manageable. But as their relationship deepened, so did Joseph's insecurities. He doubted his worth and questioned his ability to provide, which led to frequent arguments about money and gender roles within their relationship.

Nessa considered herself a traditionalist, yet her highly successful career often clashed with these values. She longed for a man who could be the breadwinner, but she always ended up footing the bill. She would have gladly submitted to a partner with the intelligence and ambition to lead their future family, yet she found herself mending the lives of grown men instead.

Despite Joseph's financial instability and lack of leadership, Nessa had focused on his looks and his undying love for her.

While physical attraction and love are important, building a relationship solely on these factors proved insufficient for her.

Nessa grappled with the reality of wearing the pants in their home. Why did she keep attracting men who made her feel this way? As she stood by the closed door, she began to wonder if she was the problem.

## **MATERNAL PROTAGONISM**

Some women are natural nurturers. They have what I call *Maternal Protagonism* - an inner drive to care, to give, to lead with love. For some, it comes from growing up in a home full of warmth. For others, it's born from the lack of it. Either way, that early experience shapes how they love later in life.

A woman who was loved deeply as a child often grows into a woman who gives that same kind of love to everyone she meets. But a woman who didn't receive enough of it tends to crave love so much that she demands nothing less than a full pour from her partner. Her nurturing spirit becomes both her strength and her weakness.

This instinct to love deeply and take charge can spill into her romantic life. She becomes the problem-solver, the caretaker, the one who makes sure everything runs smoothly. There's beauty in that kind of love - but also danger. Because when a woman starts to treat her man like her son, it can shift the balance of the relationship.

When her nurturing becomes overbearing, he starts to feel like a child being managed instead of a partner being respected.

And if he's not emotionally mature enough to handle that kind of love, he might shut down or pull away.

The effect depends on the type of man she's dealing with. If he carries Father Aura, he may feel challenged by her control. If he carries Son Aura, he'll likely cling to her, loving the comfort of her guidance.

A man with Father Aura sees himself as the leader and protector. He wants a partner, not a parent. If her nurturing crosses into control, it threatens his sense of authority. But a man with Son Aura seeks a woman who can take care of him. He thrives off her direction, her reassurance, her structure. He may love her deeply - but his love is reactive. When she pulls back, he pulls back too.

The healthiest pairing is when both the man and the woman operate on equal ground - Brother Aura and Sister Aura. Neither tries to parent the other. They lift each other up, share accountability, and draw strength from a higher source - whether that's faith, purpose, or shared goals.

When that balance is missing, things fall apart. If she gives too much, she feels drained. If he takes too much, he stops growing.

A woman with Maternal Protagonism often attracts men who depend on her love to survive, not realizing she's also feeding their dependency.

These are the men I call emotionally dependent - they don't just want love, they need it to function. They rely on her structure the same way a child depends on their mother's hand. She fills out the forms, makes the appointments, pays the bills - not because he asked her to, but because she can't stand to see him fail.

But what happens when she stops doing it? Everything starts falling apart - not because he can't, but because he never had to. Her love becomes his safety net, and his dependency becomes her burden.

Many women with this instinct stay in these cycles because of two things: a need to feel needed, and a fear of being left. If she's ever been abandoned - by a father, a parent, or a partner - control becomes her way to prevent it from happening again. She tells herself that if she handles everything, he'll have no reason to leave.

But control disguised as love is still control. And when love turns into management, connection fades.

True love doesn't need to be micromanaged. It's nurtured, not supervised. Giving care is powerful - but only when it's balanced with allowing him to stand on his own two feet.

## Addicted To Fixing Men

Some women don't just fall in love with men - they fall in love with the potential of men. The act of building gives them purpose. Watching something broken transform into something beautiful makes them feel alive. It's the same instinct that makes her rearrange her home, nurture her plants, or paint her walls - but this time, the project is human.

That desire to create and improve is part of womanhood itself. Since childhood, she's been preparing for it - playing house, dressing dolls, pretending to run homes and care for families. So when she grows up, that creativity and caretaking often shift from playtime to real life. And when she meets a man who's struggling or lost, she sees an opportunity to build.

She starts small: helping with his legal issues, paying a bill or two, updating his wardrobe, or polishing his image. She becomes his motivation, his manager, and his comfort. She tells herself she's helping him "reach his potential." But over time, she realizes that she's pouring all of her energy into a man who isn't pouring anything back.

He loves what she gives, but he doesn't grow from it. Because she's building him on the outside - the clothes, the job, the appearance - while his inner drive stays exactly the same. He's an old car with a new paint job. It looks nice, but it still won't get far.

The truth is, she can't build a man who doesn't want to build himself. And no amount of effort can replace his ambition. It's like winning the lottery - you can get lucky with money, but if you never learned how to earn it, you won't know how to keep it. The same goes for love. If a man never learned how to lead or improve his own life, he'll eventually lose everything she tried to give him.

Her biggest mistake is believing that loyalty equals transformation - that because she stood by him, he'll suddenly "get it." But love doesn't rewrite a man's blueprint.

If he's not wired to grow, he won't.

The only real way to help a man is by guiding him toward the tools he needs to fix himself. You can't fill out his job applications, take his classes, or manage his dreams. You can point him toward the opportunity, but he has to walk through the door.

Think of it like this:
- **Step 1:** Recognize the problem.
- **Step 2:** Show him where to find the tools.
- **Step 3:** Let him do the work.
- **Step 4:** Offer support when he gets stuck.

You can hand him the map, but you can't take the journey for him. If you do, he won't value the destination - because he didn't earn it.

The problem is, women with nurturing hearts often believe they can inspire change through love alone. They think, "If I love him right, he'll want to do better." But the truth is, if he's not hungry for growth, your love becomes his comfort zone instead of his motivation.

You can be the best meal in the restaurant, but if he isn't hungry, he won't eat.

That's why helping becomes harmful when it replaces accountability. Real support doesn't mean doing it for him - it means standing beside him while he learns to do it himself. Because a man who doesn't build with you will eventually make you feel like you're carrying him. And no matter how strong your love is, you can't *save* a man who's comfortable being *saved.*

## Failing With A Loser

Many women ask themselves, "Why do I always end up with a man who can't get it together?" The answer usually isn't bad luck - it's misplaced focus. You're looking at his potential instead of his reality.

When you first meet a man, depending on where you are emotionally after your last relationship, you might overlook his flaws. And if you do notice them, you tell yourself, "That's fixable." You convince yourself that once you love him enough, once he feels safe enough, he'll change. But what you're really doing is signing up for a job, not a relationship.

In the beginning, you save mental notes - the small things he'll *"grow out of,"* the habits you'll *"help him break."* You believe that love will make him level up. But over time, you discover he's not leveling up at all. He's staying the same, and you're doing all the work.

At some point, you realize you're not assisting him - you're trying to change him. And that's where the problem starts. Because trying to change a man who's not ready to grow is like watering dead grass. You're pouring life into something that doesn't want to live.

Sometimes, women overlook these flaws and walk blindly into a relationship, especially during what I call the Infatuation Stage. In that stage, emotions are high and logic is low. You only see what you want to see.

But if you fall in love before you see his flaws, the reality check hits hard. Trying to separate two hearts that are already tied together is painful. You end up exhausted - either working overtime to fix him, learning to live with him as he is, or packing your bags and admitting you misjudged him.

Here's the truth: A man's potential is only as valuable as his willingness to reach it. You can't build a future with *"what could be."* You can only build with what is.

If he doesn't want to grow, love won't make him. And if you keep trying to fix him, love will only make you tired.

## Who Is the Alpha Female

Being an alpha female comes with both power and pressure. She leads. She executes. She gets things done. But that same drive that makes her successful in business can make love complicated.

See, leadership often comes with loneliness. You'd think that in a world full of beta males, it would be easy for the alpha female to find someone to match her - but it's not that simple. The real challenge comes when she wants an alpha male. Naturally, an alpha seeks another alpha. She wants the best, and the best often wants control too. That creates friction.

When two alphas meet, it's like fire meeting fire - beautiful when contained, but destructive if not managed properly.

Now, here's the thing: not every man who walks away from an alpha woman is weak. Some alpha males know that pairing with her might create constant tension. They respect her energy but recognize that not every powerful connection is the right one.

The male lion knows when to fight and when to rest. He understands that not every roar deserves a response. Likewise, some men understand that dating an alpha female can be rewarding, but only if the balance of energy is right.

On the other hand, beta males often feel intimidated by her. Her ambition exposes their insecurities. Her dominance highlights their lack of drive. She doesn't intend to emasculate him - her mere presence does. Because when she speaks, he hears accountability. When she succeeds, he feels comparison.

The alpha female doesn't always realize that she forces reflection. She makes a man question where he stands, what he's achieved, and what he's capable of. A beta male who's not secure in himself will see her as a threat instead of an inspiration.

Now, let's talk about the dynamics.

### Alpha Female with Beta Male

A beta male can work with an alpha female - but it depends more on her than him. She has to see his value, not his status. She has to respect his quiet strength even if it doesn't roar like hers.

If she truly wants peace, she must learn patience. Understand that his happiness might not look like hers. His drive might not be fueled by competition or money. If he's content but supportive, that still has value.

She must also be sure he's not holding her back. A healthy beta male finds joy in her success because he sees it as their success. He supports her dreams, balances her energy, and reminds her to breathe.

### Beta Male with Alpha Female

His responsibility is to maintain his identity. He must bring something to the table other than compliance. She doesn't want a pet - she wants a partner. If he can be her calm in chaos, her structure in uncertainty, she'll respect him. But if he becomes dependent on her drive, she'll eventually lose attraction.

He must grow too. The best way to love an alpha woman is to evolve beside her.

A stagnant man can't hold the attention of a woman constantly in motion.

### Alpha on Alpha

Now, when two alphas meet and it works, it's magic. The problem is it rarely works for long without balance. Think of two powerful people building empires. They often collide because both are used to leading. Ego, pride, and competition can slowly erode the love if they don't learn to submit. Not to each other, but to the love itself.

Submitting to love isn't weakness. It's maturity. When you submit to love, you're saying, "We are on the same team." You're pouring energy into the bond, not the battle.

The alpha female has to remember that her strength is in her fluidity. She can be powerful and still soft. She can lead and still love. Feminine energy isn't submission to a man, it's connection to purpose.

A lioness doesn't hunt because she's weak; she hunts because she's capable. Her purpose is nourishment, not dominance. The same goes for the alpha woman. Her purpose is to build love, not control it.

When an alpha female finds a man who stays grounded in his masculine frame - steady, empathetic, confident, she can finally rest in her feminine. That's the balance every alpha woman needs: a man strong enough to lead, wise enough to listen, and soft enough to love.

## THE BREAD WINNERS

Being the breadwinner in a relationship carries weight - real weight. It comes with expectations, stress, and pride all mixed together. Whoever earns the most money in the home often feels an invisible pressure to perform, to maintain, to provide. But that sense of responsibility can also come with a sense of importance, even superiority, if not kept in check.

When a woman is the breadwinner, she must tread carefully not to slip into a parental role. The goal is partnership, not parenting. Money should never be used as proof of who loves more or who's more valuable. If love were measured by income, millionaires would automatically love deeper than working-class couples-and we all know that's not true. Love isn't about the size of a wallet; it's about the size of the effort.

Let's look at this from a real-life example instead.

*Name:* Byron
*Salary:* $1.5 million/year
*Gift:* New Purse - $9,000

*Name:* Shawn
*Salary:* $45,000/year
*Gift:* Car Repair - $4,000

Which gift means more? The answer depends on the emotion and sacrifice behind it, not the price tag. A $4,000 car repair from a man making $45K a year might carry more love and sacrifice than a $9,000 purse from a millionaire. Real value is emotional, not financial.

That's why being financially ahead doesn't give anyone permission to slack off in the love department. Throwing money at a relationship never fixes its cracks; it only covers them temporarily.

In most relationships, one person will naturally make more money than the other. That's normal. What matters is how both people handle it.

Are financial responsibilities shared evenly, or has one partner taken on the provider role while the other supports in different ways-through home management, emotional care, or family duties? Every relationship is its own system, and both parties need to understand their roles clearly.

If you live together, talk about money early.

Don't assume that because he paid the internet bill last month, he'll automatically pay it again. Don't assume that because she bought groceries twice in a row, she'll always do it. Habits without verbal agreements can cause misunderstandings. You can't hold someone accountable for a role they never agreed to.

Finances should be discussed as part of your team plan. You're not just building a house-you're building a system. When you understand each other's spending habits, strengths, and weaknesses, you can create a rhythm that works for both of you.

Remember, being the breadwinner doesn't put you above your partner - it just means you have a different function in the relationship. Love doesn't rank people by their paycheck. It measures them by their presence, their reliability, and the peace they bring into your life.

# **FINANCIALLY INSECURE MEN**

In today's world, more and more women are becoming the main earners in their homes. Because of that, many men now find themselves in situations where their woman is the one providing most of the stability. Some men are perfectly fine with this, while others secretly feel embarrassed or uneasy about it.

1. **The man who accepts it.**

This type of man sees himself as the receiver and his woman as the provider. In his mind, the love, support, and care he gives in other areas - like being there emotionally or satisfying her sexually - makes up for what he doesn't bring financially. That's how he keeps his pride intact while being comfortable with her taking the lead in money matters.

Women who are happy in this kind of setup usually aren't looking for a provider - they're looking for peace. She values how he makes her feel more than what's in his wallet. Maybe he helps calm her after stressful days, gives her comfort, and brings emotional balance to her life. In these relationships, both partners bring something valuable to the table, even if what they bring isn't equal in dollars.

2. **The man who accepts it, but she doesn't.**

Now, this is where things start to clash. You have a man who's comfortable being the receiver, but his woman deep down wants someone who can meet her on her financial level. That gap in mindset can create silent tension between them.

You might ask, *"Why would a woman stay with or even choose a man who doesn't meet her financial standards?"* The answer isn't always simple. Sometimes, when she first met him, she wasn't who she is now. Maybe she's grown - started a new business, got a raise, or found success she didn't have before. Her situation changed, but he didn't. So even though her love for him hasn't faded, her new reality may cause her to desire a partner who's more aligned with where she's headed.

That doesn't mean they've fallen out of love - it might just mean she's outgrown the version of him she met. And while financial growth can create distance, mental or spiritual growth can create even deeper separation. When one person evolves and the other doesn't, the bond weakens. If they're truly "one," they'll grow together - but if not, the gap only gets wider.

It's not always a dealbreaker, though. If she's patient and gives him space to grow, he may catch up. But many times, these inner and financial growths don't happen at the same pace. Some people even believe that a lack of mental and spiritual growth is the very reason financial growth never happens.

3. **The man who struggles with it.**

The third kind of man is the one who just can't handle being in that position. He might not say it, but deep down he feels less of a man. For him, financial insecurity isn't just about money - it's about what it represents. If he can't provide, he questions his value.

When a man sees his woman paying all the bills or living a lifestyle he can't maintain, it can hit his pride hard. You might not see a problem with it, but inside, he's battling feelings of inadequacy. That internal war can show up as frustration, distance, or even self-sabotage.

This is especially true for traditional men who were raised to believe that a man's job is to be the provider. When they can't live up to that, it eats at them. They start doubting their manhood and pulling away emotionally. Some even end relationships because they'd rather leave than face the feeling of failure.

If paying the bills defines what being a man means to him, not being able to do so can drive him crazy. And if he doesn't figure out how to fix it, he might end up ending the relationship just to escape the pressure.

A man like this needs to feel that he still has purpose in the relationship - but only if he's truly bringing something meaningful to it. There's no point in lying to make him feel good. If he contributes in emotional, physical, or practical ways, he deserves to hear that it matters. Encourage him to reach his financial goals, but also remind him that his value isn't based only on money.

But if he brings nothing - no effort, no consistency, no value - then he doesn't deserve the rewards that come from partnership. Love and respect are earned through contribution, not convenience.

## Read Nessa's story again, what do you think she should do?

# THE BOOK OF
# BRANDY

**HE'S JUST GOING THROUGH A TOUGH TIME**

**Operator:** *"Is he still in the room?"*

**Brandy:** *"No. Wait, I just heard his car start."*

**Operator:** *"Okay, stay on the line with me until officers arrive."*

**Brandy:** *"...okay."*

As she held her phone shakily to her ear, Brandy glanced down at the broken glass scattered over their wedding photo. Tonight marked the end of their eight-year marriage. Like many women, Brandy had fallen for the traditional fairytale - growing up, finding Prince Charming, buying a house, starting a family, getting a dog... maybe even a goldfish. For years, Brandy had the life most women dream of. Mason, Brandy's husband, had a gift for selling products. He made millions reviving the inventories of failing companies. Their wealth was enviable, and he had proposed to a woman in Brandy who was eager to support and love her man through it all. His words of affirmation and affection had once kept their relationship strong.

But Mason's career took a turn when companies started adopting A.I. technology to cut costs, making creators like Mason obsolete. Financial issues led him down a dark path of depression. To cope with his perceived failures, Mason began drinking heavily, and soon became verbally abusive.

Staying out late, skipping showers and speaking in pessimistic terms had become Mason's new routine. Brandy did everything she could to encourage him, to rebuild the great man she had married, but nothing worked. The man who once uplifted her now drained her. His weekly jabs at her weight and the negative energy he brought into their home were tearing their lives apart.

Feeling hopeless, Brandy contemplated having the tough conversation - divorce. Mason refused to discuss it. She wondered if there was anything she could do to save their relationship. She knew he was supposed to lead, but that didn't mean she should stand by and do nothing while he battled his demons. Questioning her own loyalty, she wondered if she should stay by his side or leave before he broke more than just glass and picture frames.

**Operator:** *"Units should be arriving now. Do you see them outside?"*

**Brandy:** *"Yes, I do. Thank you so much!"*

## **THE SAD MAN**

Depression can feel like being completely alone in a stadium full of people. You can be surrounded by family, friends, and love, yet still feel like no one truly sees you. That's why many turn to something higher than themselves - to find peace when life feels too heavy. Some people get trapped inside their own minds, unable to find a way out.

For some, the only escape seems to be at the bottom of a bottle. What others see as addiction, they see as relief - a brief break from the pain inside. Sometimes the only way they know how to quiet their mind is by harming their body, whether slowly or all at once.

There are many things that can pull someone into this dark space - losing a loved one, money problems, betrayal, or just a buildup of disappointments. What one person calls failure, another might call progress. Failure only means the goal hasn't been reached yet.

A man can easily fall into depression when he looks at his life and realizes it's nothing like he imagined it would be. He feels behind, like he's running out of time.

So how do you help a man living under that constant dark cloud? First, understand that you're going to get wet - meaning you'll feel the weight of his sadness too. But move with him at his pace, not yours. He's fighting a battle in his own mind, so don't take his moods or reactions personally. They may come out harsh, but most times they aren't truly meant for you.

However, if his behavior becomes abusive or begins to hurt you or your children, protecting your peace and safety must come first. Sometimes walking away is the best way to save both your sanity and your soul.

When you help someone with depression, don't expect a *thank you* or any signs of appreciation. In that moment, he may not be capable of showing it. Trust that your support matters and that one day, when the fog lifts, he'll understand what you did for him.

Keep in mind that money, sex, laughter, or distractions won't pull him out of it. Only time will. His mind needs time to heal, to reset, and to process what's hurting him.

Don't set deadlines or push for quick recovery. If you want to help him, just be there. Let him know that even though you can't fix his pain, you'll walk beside him through it. Tell him that he's not a burden, and mean it. Offer him your time, your understanding, and your steady love.

Something as small as a positive text every morning can remind him that he's not alone - but don't expect a reply. You may not see the results right away, but your consistency will make a difference.

In a loud world full of noise and chaos, a broken soul can still be heard. Be the quiet strength that stands by him - not for credit, but out of genuine care.

**Symptoms of Depression:**
1. Loss of interest or pleasure in usual activities.
2. Sleeping too much or too little.
3. Trouble concentrating or making decisions.
4. Restlessness or agitation.
5. Constant fatigue or low energy.
6. Feelings of guilt or worthlessness.
7. Thoughts of self-harm or suicide.
8. Major changes in appetite or weight.

## His Low Self-Esteem

A man's greatest strength often lies in his confidence. When that confidence fades, it can change everything about him. Most men want to feel respected, capable, and in control. When he loses those feelings, love alone might not be enough to bring him back. If you don't recognize what's happening, it can leave you confused and hurt by how he acts.

Many men are taught from an early age to tie their worth to their success. Society, social media, and television feed them false images of what "winning" looks like. They end up measuring themselves against unrealistic standards. Over time, that pressure chips away at their self-esteem. The truth is, only he can define what success means for him - and sometimes, he needs to be reminded of that.

You might be doing everything right - showing him love, giving him attention - yet your words could still sting if they make him feel small. Whispering his wins but shouting his failures will crush his spirit. When a man has fallen from his throne, your words hold even more power. The last thing he needs is confirmation that he's not good enough. Even when he starts to recover and seems happy again, let him have that moment. Encourage him to build on it.

And when you see him slipping, remind him that he's capable, that he just needs more time.

Men need partners who are patient and non-judgmental. The world already expects them to carry everything - to lead, to provide, to never break. And when life knocks them down, they're told to get up and smile like nothing happened. That pressure can break even the strongest man. So when his confidence cracks, your support shouldn't come in the form of pity, but in reassurance. Let him know you still see the man he's trying to be.

In relationships, women are often measured by how well they nurture; men are measured by how well they lead. But in today's world, those lines are starting to blur - and that's okay. Growth isn't about who leads or who follows; it's about walking side by side until both of you feel whole again.

## **NEGATIVE ENERGY**

Sometimes a man's energy feels so heavy that your whole body reacts when he walks in the room. You might get a headache, a knot in your stomach, or feel drained without him even saying a word. That's because energy is real - it's what we're made of - and when his energy is low, it can pull you down with it.

Everything in life has vibration. Think of energy as levels on a scale. When someone's vibration is high, they feel light, calm, confident, and full of peace. When someone's vibration is low, they carry anger, sadness, or frustration. The lower they go, the darker their world becomes. And when two people are on different energy levels, you can feel it - like two radio stations playing at the same time, both full of static.

If you're in a good space and he's not, being around him might make you feel anxious or uneasy. That's your body warning you that your energies aren't matching. It doesn't mean you don't love him - it just means you're not aligned in that moment. And if that imbalance continues for too long, it starts to affect your peace, your health, and your happiness.

You've probably noticed how anger works. When someone tries to start an argument and you stay calm, it makes them even madder. That's because they want you to meet them at their vibration. They want you to join them in that low space. But when you don't, it forces them to see how far they've fallen. The same happens with positivity - when you're full of light, it can irritate people who are living in darkness.

Being aware of your vibration is one of the most powerful forms of self-care. If you stay in negative energy long enough, you'll start to attract more of it. It's like walking through mud - every step gets heavier. But if you start climbing, even slowly, you'll notice that better things begin to show up. Blessings exist at higher frequencies, and to reach them, you have to raise your own.

Spiritually, this is what faith represents - rising above fear, anger, and pain. When you choose peace instead of pettiness, when you forgive instead of retaliate, you lift your vibration. And when your energy rises, your life follows.

Pay attention to your body when you're around him. If you constantly feel sick, tense, or uneasy, that's your body telling you his vibration is too far below yours. You can still love him, but you have to protect your peace. Sometimes, helping him means first grounding yourself - making sure you don't sink trying to save him.

A healthy relationship is one where both partners check each other's energy and bring balance when things are off. Talk about how the energy feels between you. Be honest about what you sense, and encourage him to work on it with you.

Because love without harmony becomes survival. And relationships built on survival eventually burn out.

Arguments will happen, but peace comes from how you solve them. Don't just hope he'll change - help create an environment where he wants to rise with you. That's how two people truly grow together.

## HEALING HIS ANXIETY

You don't really *cure* anxiety - you learn from it. In a strange way, anxiety can be the very thing that shapes a man into something stronger. It's like a sculptor's chisel, carving away fear and weakness until only the best version of him remains. The problem is, most people see anxiety as punishment instead of a teacher.

Anxiety comes to shake things up when life becomes too routine or comfortable. Growth doesn't happen in comfort. Every great story has a struggle, and anxiety is often part of that plot. It forces a man to look at the things he's been ignoring - his fears, his habits, his truth.

The secret to easing anxiety is to stop fighting it. The more you resist it, the stronger it becomes. When you accept it and let it pass through you, it loses its power. Tell him that when he feels panic coming, it's not his enemy - it's just his body reacting to fear. And fear, once faced, always fades.

If your man deals with anxiety, he might act distant, sad, or even shut down emotionally. You'll notice it affecting his sleep, his patience, or your intimacy. But only he can calm the storm - you can't fix it for him. What you can do is remind him that he's safe, that this moment will pass, and that no one has ever died from an anxiety attack.

Sometimes sharing a story helps him feel less alone. I remember my first anxiety attack back in 2015. I had just quit smoking, ended a toxic relationship, and released my first book - all things that should've felt like progress. Instead, my body went into chaos. My heart raced for no reason. I couldn't catch my breath. It wasn't until I stopped fearing the attacks and started welcoming them that they began to lose their grip. I'd say, *"Alright, come on in, let's get this over with."* That shift - from fear to acceptance - gave me back control.

When a man begins to accept his anxiety, it becomes less of a monster and more of a reminder. It tells him when he's overwhelmed, when he's carrying too much, or when he's not living in alignment.

If you love a man going through this, encourage him to workout, eat better, sleep more, stay physically active, manage stress. Remind him to slow down, breathe, and focus on what he can control. Remind him that even though the anxiety feels like it's tearing him apart, it's actually shaping him into something new.

When he finally comes out on the other side, he'll realize he was never broken - he was just being rebuilt.

## THE LOST MAN

When a man loses his purpose, he loses his sense of self. It's like watching someone wander through life with no map, no compass, and no destination. You can see the confusion in his eyes, hear the emptiness in his words, and feel the heaviness in the air around him. Living with a man who's lost like this can drain you too, especially if you're constantly trying to pull him out of his darkness.

You can't let his struggle pull you under. When his energy becomes negative, it will challenge every ounce of strength you have. But if you stay positive, you'll grow through it too. In some ways, his loss of direction can shape both of you - testing your patience, your boundaries, and your will to keep peace in chaos.

If you see him giving up on himself - not trying, not planning, not even caring - it may be time to step back. Sometimes distance is the only thing that helps a person find clarity. Let him know that you still care, but explain that you can't keep pouring into someone who's refusing to fill their own cup. And if children are involved, you must protect your energy for them, because they need at least one stable light in the house.

For a man who's truly lost, faith might be his only rescue. Whether that faith is in God, the universe, or something beyond him, he needs to believe there's still a path meant for him - even if he can't see it yet.

You can guide him, pray for him, and remind him of who he once was. But ultimately, he must want to find his way back.

**Read Brandy's story again, is there anything they could have tried before they got to this point?**

# THE BOOK OF
# ASHLEY

**HE DID IT BECAUSE HE LOVES ME**

Staring into the bathroom mirror, Ashley examined her bruises. The blood smeared across her lips felt both foreign and familiar. With trembling fingertips, she lightly traced the swollen eyes Jonathan had left her with. This wasn't the first time he had laid hands on her, and she feared it wouldn't be the last.

She knew this feeling all too well, often dismissing these brutal moments as mere misunderstandings. Sometimes, she even blamed herself, concocting excuses to defend him. *"He grew up in a violent home." "I provoked him." "He's just possessive because he loves me so much."* Ashley viewed Jonathan's abusive behavior as *their* problem, not just *his*. They skillfully avoided questions, hiding the truth beneath layers of makeup. She saw them as one; his issues were hers. She believed in taking the good with the bad, thinking no one was perfect.

His abuse didn't start with his fists; it began with his words. The mental manipulation and degrading comments bled into her public life. Teasing her about her weight gain, constantly questioning her intelligence - these eroded her peace of mind, weakening her confidence and strengthening his control.

Her close friends would say, *"Ashley, we can see your bruises. We hear how he talks to you. Why won't you leave him?"* She never had an answer. Her response was always to downplay the situation. To Ashley, love was complicated and a concept her friends couldn't understand. So, their relationship continued, a cycle of pain and excuses.

What twists a man's mind to believe that violence is an answer? What sense does it make to break down the woman who holds you up? How do these relationships endure?

# SEEK HELP

Before we proceed further, it is crucial to address this pressing matter. If you have recently experienced physical abuse within your relationship, I strongly urge you to seek immediate assistance from local authorities. Your safety and well-being are paramount, and prompt action can be lifesaving. If contacting law enforcement feels daunting, there are dedicated Domestic Violence hotlines available to provide guidance and support tailored to your specific situation. **Please** prioritize your safety and **seek help** without hesitation.

For anyone who finds themselves becoming an abuser, **please seek** the professional **help** you need. If you ever feel you have crossed the line, take responsibility as an adult. Ignoring it will only make things worse.

## MENTAL & EMOTIONAL ABUSE

# CONTROL FREAK

Some men grow up believing they're supposed to control everything their woman does. They think leadership means ownership. But a relationship should be a union - not a dictatorship.

Here are signs of a controlling personality:

1. Micromanaging your every move and not trusting you to handle things yourself.
2. Setting impossible standards, then punishing you for not meeting them.
3. Refusing to share responsibilities because he thinks only he can do things "the right way."
4. Always insisting that his way is the only way.
5. Constantly criticizing or judging your decisions.
6. Becoming upset when plans change or things don't go exactly as expected.
7. Dominating conversations or making choices for you without asking.

8. Refusing to bend or compromise on rules and routines.
9. Demanding order and structure to an extreme degree.
10. Using guilt, fear, or emotional pressure to control your behavior.

Some men even use religion as a weapon - quoting scripture to justify dominance or make you feel guilty for not obeying. True spirituality brings peace and growth, not manipulation or shame.

This type of man confuses fear with strength. Deep down, he's afraid - of losing control, of being exposed, of feeling powerless. To hide that scared little boy inside, he projects his fear onto you. Every insult, every restriction, every demand is really a reflection of his own insecurity.

But he'll never stop until he faces the real source of his pain. Until he fixes that, the faucet keeps running - pouring pain onto you while trying to fill the emptiness inside himself.

## BREAKING HER CONFIDENCE

His goal is simple - make you doubt yourself. Because if you don't believe in your own strength, you won't leave him. He withholds compliments, minimizes your achievements, or subtly criticizes your appearance.

Compliments from a stranger can feel nice, but hearing them from the one you love hits differently. So when the person who once made you feel beautiful suddenly stops or starts tearing you down, it cuts deeper than words from anyone else.

A man who wants control will chip away at your confidence piece by piece. Sometimes he does it intentionally, sometimes out of habit. Either way, it works - as long as you stay unsure of yourself, you'll keep trying to earn his approval.

But your worth isn't defined by his opinion. His idea of beauty, value, or success comes from his own upbringing, beliefs, and insecurities - not from truth. What he sees in you says more about his mind than your reflection.

When he tries to tear you down, see it as motivation. Let his words sharpen you, not break you. If he points out something true, grow from it. If it's false, prove him wrong by living better. Either way, his attempt to weaken you will only make you stronger. Because without realizing it, he's shaping the woman strong enough to walk away from him.

## **THE FINANCIAL CAGE**

In traditional households, the man provides, and the woman manages the home. But when that structure turns into control, it becomes a trap. Financial abuse is one of the most powerful ways to dominate someone - if he controls your income, he controls your freedom.

Some men disguise this as protection: *"You don't have to work; I'll take care of you."* That might sound loving at first, but when it comes with restrictions - like forbidding you to work, hiding financial information, or keeping all accounts in his name - it becomes dangerous.

It's perfectly fine if one partner earns more or handles most of the finances. What's not fine is when the other has no access to money, no understanding of the bills, and no safety plan if things go wrong.

Both partners should have some level of financial awareness. Even if he manages the money, you should know where the accounts are, how to access them, and what's happening with your shared income. In emergencies - even if that emergency is escaping abuse - you should have the ability to survive independently.

Trust is good, but blind trust can be deadly. A true partnership means transparency - no hidden accounts, no secret properties, no unspoken debts. You both deserve financial peace and equal protection.

## **LOVE DROUGHT**

People often talk about women using intimacy to get what they want - but men do it too, through love and affection. When a man withholds his touch, attention, or emotional warmth to punish or manipulate you, that's emotional control.

When he's upset and refuses to talk, he may pull away instead, making you anxious and desperate for connection. Once you start chasing his affection, he knows he has control. This back-and-forth becomes a game - the more you comply, the more power he gains.

The way out is to break the cycle. Confront it calmly. Ask him to communicate. Tell him you want to work through things with words, not silence. Show him that emotional withdrawal doesn't solve problems - it just creates distance.

But if he refuses to speak, you have two choices: patience or power. You can give him space while keeping your peace, or you can mirror his distance until he realizes you won't chase him. That approach is risky and often signals the end - but it also exposes whether he values control more than connection.

Never let anyone starve you of love to make you submit. You deserve affection that's consistent, not conditional.

### **PHYSICAL ABUSE**

# Hands On

There are many reasons some men become violent, but one truth stands out - that anger has usually lived inside them for years. It often starts in childhood. A boy who grows up watching or experiencing abuse learns that pain is how power is shown. By the time he becomes a man, that pain is buried so deep that it controls him. What you're seeing isn't new behavior; it's an old wound that never healed.

Abuse rewires the brain. When a child's first example of love also brings fear, he grows up confusing control with care.

That's why therapy is often the only real path toward change - he has to learn to express pain with words instead of his hands.

Many people were never taught conflict resolution. They don't know how to process anger or disappointment in healthy ways. Mix that with a violent upbringing, and the result can be disastrous.

It's common for women to be drawn to men with a "tough edge." The protective, assertive energy feels safe - at first. It's natural to want a man who can defend his home and family. But when that same energy belongs to a man whose emotions never matured past childhood, it becomes dangerous. The aggression that once felt protective now turns inward - aimed at you.

Substance abuse often fuels this behavior. Alcohol and drugs can lower inhibitions and bring out buried rage. They turn that inner war loose. That's why it's so important for men to recognize addiction early. Some of them don't realize that the person who surfaces under the influence is someone even they don't know - someone who shouldn't be trusted.

Just like anxiety, addiction must be separated from identity. It's something he battles, not something he is.

But until he sees it that way, the addiction will run his life and destroy everything around him.

## SHE LIKES BAD BOYS

Many women mistake emotional instability for strength. The "street guy," the "tough guy," or the man who's quick to fight - these types may seem fearless and protective, but what you're really seeing is a lack of emotional control.

A man who can be triggered by something as small as a bump in a club or a rude comment is dangerous - not strong. His pride becomes a ticking time bomb. And when you're with him, you're living inside the blast zone.

Men like this take risks in every part of life. They gamble their safety, their freedom, and often, their family's peace of mind. While they may have good intentions to protect their loved ones, their reactions usually put everyone in greater danger.

Many of these men live surrounded by drugs and chaos. That environment fuels their ego and aggression. When you mix substances with a fragile emotional state, it becomes a recipe for violence.

True strength doesn't roar - it reasons. A real man knows how to walk away before his emotions take over. He values peace more than pride. He uses words to de-escalate, not fists to dominate. He won't risk his family's future for a stranger's respect.

A healthy man knows when to fight, but more importantly, he knows when not to.

## Ego Is God

Physical abuse doesn't always come from loud, aggressive men. Sometimes, it hides behind charm and calmness. He looks put-together on the outside - polite, respectable, even spiritual. But behind closed doors, he's consumed by ego.

This man doesn't just want control; he wants worship. When he feels small, he inflates himself by shrinking you. He disciplines you with anger because he confuses dominance with authority. In his twisted logic, hurting you reaffirms his manhood.

A man ruled by ego cannot love anyone. His only mission is to protect the image he built in his own mind. When God is absent, ego becomes his god. And when ego is god, destruction follows.

Some of these men even sit in church pews on Sundays, quoting scripture they don't live by. They think faith is a costume, not a lifestyle. But true godliness never controls - it guides. It doesn't demand fear; it creates peace.

Abuse gives these men a temporary high - a sense of power. But when that high fades, shame creeps in. That's when you'll hear the apologies, the promises, the tears. But unless they deal with their ego and trauma, the cycle will repeat.

When he feels like he's losing control, he'll lash out harder. If you start to rise - emotionally, spiritually, or financially - he'll try to pull you back down. In his mind, your growth exposes his weakness. And he'll do anything to cover it up.

No woman deserves to live in fear of a man she loves. No love is worth losing yourself.

## **SAFE EXIT**

If you ever find yourself in a violent or dangerous relationship, you must have a plan - not just an idea, but a step-by-step escape route. Abusive people thrive on control, and when they sense they're losing it, they can become unpredictable. Planning your exit ahead of time can save your life.

Start by creating a safety plan. Choose a few trusted people you can contact in an emergency - friends, relatives, coworkers, or even a neighbor. Establish a "safe word" or short phrase that only they understand, something you can say in a text or phone call to signal that you need help immediately.

Identify a safe place where you can go at any hour - somewhere he doesn't know about or can't access. This could be a family member's home, a shelter, or even a public location like a police station. Keep a bag packed with essentials - ID, cash, credit card, keys, medications, important documents, and a change of clothes. Hide it somewhere easy to grab but hard for him to find.

If you share children, include them in the plan in a way that won't endanger them. Teach them how to dial 911 and what to say. Make sure they know never to get in the middle of a physical fight.

If you drive, plan different routes to and from work or school. Abusers often monitor routines, so changing your route or schedule can protect you. Tell someone at work or school what's happening so they can help if something looks off.

There are resources that can help you build your plan safely and privately. One of the most trusted is The National Domestic Violence Hotline - available 24/7 at thehotline.org or by phone at **1-800-799-SAFE (7233)**. They can help you create a detailed plan and connect you with local shelters, legal services, and counselors.

Remember, you are not overreacting. You are not weak. You are protecting your life and possibly the lives of your children. The decision to leave can be terrifying but staying with someone who's already shown you violence is far more dangerous.

Your safety comes first - always.

## POST-TRAUMATIC AWARENESS

Even after escaping an abusive relationship, the damage can linger long after the bruises fade. Emotional wounds don't heal on command - they take time, patience, and intentional care.

Many survivors experience ongoing anxiety, flashbacks, or emotional triggers that surface unexpectedly. This is part of what's known as Post-Traumatic Stress Disorder (PTSD).

You might find yourself avoiding certain places, songs, or even scents that remind you of the past. You might wake up from nightmares or suddenly feel unsafe for no clear reason. These reactions don't mean you're weak - they mean your mind is still trying to protect you. When those moments come, grounding yourself can help.

Try asking simple questions:

- *What's happening right now?*
- *Who am I with?*
- *What do I see and hear?*
- *How does my body feel in this moment?*

Bringing your focus back to the present helps signal to your brain that the danger is over.

Depression after trauma is common, too. Some people isolate themselves, while others may overwork or distract themselves just to avoid thinking about the past.

Healing doesn't always look peaceful - sometimes it's messy, and that's okay.

It's also important to remember that their abusive behavior was a reflection of them, not you. Their actions came from their own insecurities, fears, or mental issues - not because of anything you did. That's not your burden to carry. Never try to "fix" or confront an abuser after you've left. Doing so only reopens old wounds and can put you in danger. Your responsibility is not to heal them - it's to protect your peace and rebuild your sense of self.

If you find your emotions becoming overwhelming, consider therapy or support groups for survivors of abuse. Talking about your experiences can be painful at first, but it's one of the most powerful steps toward taking your power back.

Healing takes time, but every small step - every moment you choose peace over chaos - is progress. You survived something heavy. You deserve to breathe again.

## Read Ashley's story again, what do you think she should do

# THE BOOK OF ARIANA

**DOES HE EVEN CARE**

With phone in hand, Ariana hurried upstairs to her bedroom.

"*Where is it?*" She mumbled under her breath.

A faint voice from the phone said, "*You can just call me back when you charge it.*"

**Ariana:** *"No!"*
**Bryson:** *"Ok."*

Bryson and Ariana had been dating for exactly 5 months, 3 weeks, and 2 days - to quote Ariana's count. For her, it had been a time of joy and completeness; she had finally gotten the man she wanted. She felt comfortable with him, allowing her vulnerable self to *be free*. She embraced every path their journey took.

Their relationship was young in nature. They dealt within their lower selves and sex was at the forefront of their connection. This immediate attraction suited Bryson perfectly, while Ariana was newer to the casual sex dating scene. Bryson navigated these waters with ease.

After months of happy moments, Ariana's feelings for Bryson deepened, and so did her expectations. She hoped his feelings would grow as hers had. However, she quickly learned that love doesn't always evolve in sync.

As her love for Bryson grew, she began to crave more from him. She wanted to plan a future together, but Bryson wasn't ready. He wasn't there for love; he wasn't there to build something lasting. And although she hadn't been either at the beginning, things changed for her.

She started discussing their future, as a test to see if he

envisioned the same things she did. Bryson remained noncommittal. She planned dates and weekend getaways, but Bryson wasn't available.

Some might wonder why Ariana continued to invest in a relationship where she didn't get much in return. Bryson was the first man to genuinely make her happy, at least when they were together. But when apart, uncertainty clouded her security. The security she feels in his arms is gone when he's no longer around. When it was good, it was *great*; when it was bad, it was *terrifying*.

Ariana didn't want to seem like a nag, so she held her tongue. She didn't even know if she had the right to question him since he never labeled their relationship as heading toward something serious - they were just enjoying their time together as he put it.

Bryson was a wanted man among women in the city, and Ariana almost felt privileged that he showed interest in her. She didn't want to ruin a good thing, so she kept quiet.

It wasn't until their one year *"situationship"* mark that things took a turn. Ariana expected some acknowledgment, perhaps a gift or special time together. But Bryson didn't even mention the day. Disappointed, she sent him a long text and he responded.....

**Ariana:** *"I'm really disappointed and saddened by the lack of care you've shown me lately. I've kept quiet about many things I've noticed, not wanting to make a fuss over trivial matters. But if I don't say anything, it will keep happening, and that's not fair to me. Today was our one-year anniversary, and I didn't hear from you. I waited all day to hear from you. If you're not into this like I am, just say so, and I'll leave you alone."*

**Bryson:** *"Anniversary is crazy."*
**Ariana:** *"You know what I meant. Is that all you got from that?"*
**Bryson:** *"I understand you're upset we didn't spend time on our 'anniversary.' I've never really celebrated things like this. Maybe if it was a one-year anniversary of a relationship or marriage, I'd pay more attention to it."*
**Ariana:** *"So what are we?"*
**Bryson:** *... (He paused from texting for a moment)*
**Ariana:** *"???"*
**Bryson:** *"My bad, I stepped away from my phone."*
**Bryson:** *"I'd say we're two people who are extremely happy*

together and miss each other when we're apart. During that separation, we let negative thoughts cloud our minds until we reunite."

**Ariana:** *"Do you even like me?"*

**Bryson:** *"Probably more than I should lol."*

**Ariana:** *"Whatever. When am I going to see you then?"*

**Bryson:** *"I'll come over tomorrow."*

**Ariana:** *"Ok, bae."*

**Bryson:** *"♥"*


And around...and around...and around...they went.

## THE NONCHALANT GUY

Have you ever dated a man who seems more like a robot than a partner - someone who never seems to care about anything? Some men are naturally aloof, while others only act that way depending on the person they're with. This means that their behavior can shift based on the situation. When a man starts dating, he usually gauges early on how important the connection is. The less important the connection feels to him, the less effort he puts in. On the other hand, the more he values it, the more involved and attentive he becomes.

That's why women are often right to be concerned when a man shows little effort. Now, I don't believe a man should drop everything in his life to focus only on you in the early stages. He doesn't need to "read your mind" or buy you gifts just to prove his interest, like social media might suggest. But I do believe that a man should be observant and gradually show through his actions that he's learning what you like and what matters to you.

Sadly, some men maintain long-term relationships without ever being attentive. Before getting into the deeper side of "learning your partner," there are simple, basic actions that show he's paying attention to your life. Taking out the trash when he's over, changing a beeping smoke detector, or replacing a light bulb - these small acts show awareness and care. They might seem minor, but they reveal what kind of man you're dealing with.

Then there are the more thoughtful gestures - like putting air in your tires, washing your car, or handling your gas or oil changes. These are the kinds of things a man who genuinely cares will notice and take care of. He doesn't have to know you deeply to recognize these needs; he just has to be tuned in to your well-being. A man who's a good asset to a household and interested in you will make it his business to take care of those things. It's not a grand gesture - it's consistency.

But for all of this to matter, your relationship must have a foundation built for growth. If your connection started off centered on sex, then you may have entered a situation meant for pleasure, not partnership. Don't go searching for a man in every casual encounter. If the first conversations were all about what happens in the bedroom, chances are that's all the connection will be about. He'll stay attentive only to how you please him sexually, not how he can please your heart.

Often, the detached and unbothered attitude some men display comes from what's called an "abundance mindset." These men know their value and believe many women would want them. Whether that confidence comes from their upbringing, looks, financial status, or sexual ability, they feel assured that losing you isn't the end of the world. He might not want to lose you - but if he does, he's convinced he'll recover just fine.

## Big Dick Energy

We've all heard of the term *Big Dick Energy*. For those who haven't, it refers to a man who carries himself with supreme confidence, fully aware of what he brings to the table - especially in intimate settings. Originally, the phrase was used to describe men who were well-endowed and had complete faith in their ability to satisfy their partner. But, like most popular terms, it's been borrowed and now applies to women and men alike, regardless of the original context.

A man with *BDE* usually carries a calm, controlled energy. He's laid back, grounded, and never seems to be rattled by much. That steady demeanor draws people in, especially women. To many women, his composure feels safe - it lets them relax and embrace their feminine side. In a world where many women are forced to take on masculine energy to survive, a man who radiates confidence without chaos gives them space to breathe, to soften, and to simply be.

However, there's a dark side to this energy. When it crosses the line into arrogance or cockiness, it becomes toxic. Once he starts looking down on others, thinking he's better than everyone around him, that same energy that once attracted people becomes repelling. True confidence doesn't need comparison. Having *BDE* doesn't mean you're above anyone-it simply means you know that no one is above you.

When that confidence turns dismissive - when he stops caring about your feelings or concerns, that's when ego takes over. Every time a woman praises his energy, it feeds his pride even more. Eventually, he develops a set pattern for how he treats women - a formula that's been validated time and time again. Because so many women before you accepted his behavior, he assumes you're the problem if you don't. To him, it's not his attitude that's off - it's your reaction to it.

Trying to change this type of man is nearly impossible. He doesn't believe there's anything to fix. In his mind, he has proof that his way works - because thirty-five women before you confirmed it. Half of them loved him and took what came with the package. The other half didn't care, as long as they were satisfied physically and got to feel feminine in his presence. You might just be the first to challenge his emotional absence. So in his eyes, it's thirty-five to one.

And when the scoreboard looks like that in his mind, he won't change - because to him, the math already makes sense.

## **EMOTIONALLY UNAVAILABLE**

Being with an emotionally unavailable man can feel like loving a brick wall. You pour out affection, attention, and care, yet everything seems to bounce right back at you. It's not that he's always being cruel - sometimes, he just doesn't know how to connect. His heart is present, but it's locked away.

Real connection requires emotional openness. It's not just about sex or physical touch; it's about those quiet moments where you both share what's inside. Everyone deserves a partner who can shoulder emotional weight and offer genuine comfort when life gets heavy. But when that emotional support never comes, the relationship starts to feel one-sided and draining.

Men who are emotionally disconnected tend to avoid long-term commitments. To build something lasting, they'd have to let their emotions flow - and that's exactly what they fear. They dodge deep conversations about the future and keep things surface-level to protect themselves.

A man who lacks empathy struggles to understand your pain. He may come off as dismissive or cold, even if he doesn't mean to. It's not always malicious - it's often just emotional immaturity. Without empathy, he can't truly listen or offer compassion when you need it most.

What makes this type of man so confusing is the mixed signals. One week, he's all in, calling, texting, acting committed. The next, he's distant or withdrawn. To him, the relationship is something to indulge in, not invest in. When emotions aren't involved, commitment feels like a chore, not a choice.

Often, emotionally unavailable men fill the void with multiple partners or shallow flings. Since they can't connect deeply, they substitute love with lust, mistaking one for the other. But no matter how many encounters they have, the emptiness stays.

Their detachment can also make their words sting. Because they speak from logic, not emotion, they lack the sensitivity filter most people use. This makes them seem harsh or uncaring. Over time, that emotional distance can feel like rejection.

These men also tend to resist compromise, seeing relationships as something that should run on their terms. They control the pace - when to talk, when to be distant, and when to reconnect - creating an unspoken power imbalance. It's not always intentional manipulation, but it still leaves you feeling small.

At the root of this, many emotionally unavailable men have one thing in common: pain. Some grew up without affection, guidance, or consistent love. The environment they were raised in shaped how they give/don't give - love today.

When love was scarce growing up, they learned that being cold was safer than being hurt. They built walls to protect themselves from disappointment. But those walls don't just keep pain out; they also keep love from getting in.

### The Loved Child

Children who grow up in loving homes learn early how to give and receive love. They're nurtured, encouraged, and allowed to express their emotions without fear. Because of this, they often become adults who operate from a place of compassion and understanding. Love is their natural language.

When life challenges them, they tend to see problems through a softer lens. Their instinct isn't to harm or hurt others but to heal and restore balance. That doesn't mean they never get angry or make mistakes - it just means that at their core, they're rooted in love. It's their default setting, their "factory reset."

These individuals usually lead with empathy. They're not driven by ego or the need to prove themselves; instead, they're motivated by peace and fairness. They want things to make sense emotionally, not just logically. When they see pain in others, they try to ease it. When they cause pain, they try to fix it.

But with that openness comes vulnerability. When your heart is wide open, you feel love more deeply - but you also feel pain more sharply. This is the trade-off of living from the heart: the same door that lets love in also lets pain through.

To truly experience love in its purest form, one must accept that heartbreak, disappointment, and loss may also come with it. For many, this is the hardest part of being love-centered. Still, even when hurt, they rarely let bitterness take over. Instead, they try to heal and return to that natural state of love.

This type of person brings warmth into relationships. They're usually patient, forgiving, and willing to communicate. But if their partner doesn't operate from that same emotional space, they can end up feeling used, misunderstood, or taken for granted.

Their greatest strength - their capacity for love, can also be their greatest weakness if paired with someone who doesn't know how to handle it.

### The Unloved Child

Children who grow up without real love often learn early that love hurts. Maybe they were ignored, criticized, or treated like their feelings didn't matter. Over time, they begin to see love not as comfort, but as danger. So, instead of reaching for it, they protect themselves from it.

The human mind naturally avoids pain. When love has been linked to pain, the body and mind work together to block it out. These children grow into adults who don't trust affection. They may crave love, but when it gets too close, they shut down. It's not that they don't want to love - it's that they don't know how to let it in without fearing it'll destroy them.

Instead of living from love, they live from survival. They focus on control, self-protection, and independence. To them, being vulnerable feels like weakness. They often come across as detached, guarded, or cold, when in truth, they're terrified of being hurt again.

The absence of affection during childhood teaches them that showing emotion can be dangerous. They build emotional walls, brick by brick - made from betrayal, neglect, or disappointment. Each bad experience becomes another layer of protection. Whether it was a father who left, a mother who lied, or the loss of someone they depended on, each moment reinforces the same painful message: love isn't safe.

As adults, they may enter relationships still carrying that old fear. They might keep their partner at a distance, emotionally or physically. They might struggle to say "I love you" or accept it when it's said to them. It's not rejection, it's defense.

What's important to understand is that this type of emotional unavailability doesn't come from arrogance or cruelty; it comes from trauma. It's a learned behavior that once kept them safe. To change, they must first become aware of it.

Healing begins when they realize that what once protected them is now preventing them from experiencing peace. Once that awareness forms, love can begin to chip away at the walls - slowly, patiently, consistently.

### Low Self-Esteem

Low self-esteem can quietly drain the life out of a relationship. A man who doesn't believe in himself can't truly give love because he doesn't feel he has much to give. To pour into someone else, you have to have something inside you first. When a man doubts his own worth, his cup stays empty, and what little love he tries to share often comes out mixed with insecurity and fear.

He might question your loyalty even when you've done nothing wrong. He might assume you'll leave him for someone "better." He may need constant reassurance, or he might withdraw completely to avoid rejection before it happens.

Either way, his low view of himself shapes how he treats you and how he receives your affection.

If he doesn't see value in who he is, he won't believe he deserves your love. And when someone feels undeserving, they either push love away or hold onto it too tightly. Both are symptoms of the same wound.

These insecurities can also come from past relationships that broke him down. If he was cheated on, constantly criticized, or made to feel small, he'll carry that pain into his next relationship unless he heals from it. Until he does, even your kindness can make him uneasy. He'll question your motives or assume it's temporary because deep down, he doesn't believe he's worth consistency.

True confidence isn't about ego or arrogance; it's about being secure enough to give and receive love without fear. If he's struggling with that, encourage him to rebuild himself - not for you, but for his own peace. Confidence and self-love take time, but they can be relearned.

When a man finds his sense of worth again, his love deepens. He becomes more patient, more giving, and more capable of meeting you emotionally. But until he gets there, understand that you can't fix him - you can only support him as he learns to fix himself.

## Previous Love

Fear of being hurt again makes a man hesitant to open his heart. Many women end up paying for the mistakes of women they've never even met. When a man hasn't healed from a past relationship, he often builds emotional walls - not because he doesn't care, but because he's still guarding scars that haven't fully closed.

Sometimes, his heart is still tied to someone from his past. He may not see her, text her, or even talk about her, but emotionally, he's still pouring into the memory of what they once had. In his mind, he's replaying moments, trying to make sense of how things went wrong. That energy, those lingering thoughts, keep him stuck in the past, unable to be fully present with you.

It's like trying to build a new home while secretly keeping the old one standing. He can't live in both. He must eventually decide which foundation to build on. As the saying goes, *"You can't steal second base while keeping your foot on first."*

Until he finds closure, he'll struggle to give you the love you deserve. He might pull back just when things start to feel real or sabotage the relationship before it gets too deep. It's not always intentional, it's often fear disguised as control. He's afraid of feeling the same pain again, so he avoids the kind of love that could cause it.

His heart still clings to a comfort zone that no longer exists. That familiar pain feels safer than the uncertainty of something new. But healing only begins when he faces that truth.

You can't fight the ghost of another woman. What you can do is make him aware of how his past affects his present. Then, give him space to confront it. Once he acknowledges the emotional hold that old relationship still has on him, he can finally release it and make room for something real with you.

But if he refuses to do that inner work - if he keeps replaying the past instead of building a future, you may need to take a step back. Love isn't meant to be a waiting room. It's a journey meant for two people who are ready to move forward together.

## You're the Prize?

Lately, there's been a lot of debate about who the "prize" is in a relationship. Some men claim they're the prize; some women say the same. On the surface, it might sound like harmless confidence, but beneath it, this mindset often turns into competition instead of connection.

If you believe you're the prize, it's worth asking - what does that really mean? If you're the prize, then who owns or claims you? If you say you're the prize but choose someone who doesn't treat you like one, what does that say about your choices? Value doesn't mean superiority. The truth is, in a healthy relationship, both people are the prize because both bring something valuable to the table.

Our culture often encourages rivalry instead of unity. People boast about what they bring to the relationship as if it's a contest. But a truly valuable partner doesn't need to prove it - they show it through consistency, effort, and love. Real worth doesn't have to be declared; it's demonstrated.

Yes, you may have incredible qualities - ambition, kindness, beauty, financial stability. But if you can't apply those strengths within a relationship, they lose their meaning. It's like someone having all the right tools but never building anything with them. You can have a good heart, a solid career, or even physical attraction, but if you can't communicate, compromise, or support your partner, those qualities become individual trophies, not shared treasures.

We often confuse confidence with ego. Confidence says, "I bring value, and so does my partner." Ego says, "I'm the only one who matters." The first builds love; the second destroys it.

Think about it this way: in a strong relationship, both partners lift each other up. One's success is the other's win. That's what makes a real prize - a bond where both feel equally valued.

Look at couples who truly complement each other. For example, most people assume Barack Obama is the prize because he became President. But without Michelle's strength, balance, and influence, that story wouldn't be complete. In their relationship, both shine *equally* because they understand that love is a partnership, not a pedestal.

In the end, a healthy, functioning relationship itself *is* the prize - not one person over the other. Because when both people recognize each other's value and work together toward something greater, that's when love truly wins.

# Read Ariana's story again, what do you think she should do?

# THE BOOK OF
# HALLE

**LEAVE THE KIDS ALONE**

Halle and Maurice's eight-year rollercoaster of a relationship hit a devastating crest when they finally called it quits. Although the decision to separate was mutual, the disappointment and shame were not. Halle was a prideful woman who spoke highly of her man; some would say she placed him on a pedestal. He was always chasing a bag, in the streets regularly, which is one of the many reasons she loved him so much. He made sure she was financially secure. He was her protection from life's ills. So, you can imagine the pain she endured when she found out he was sleeping with her best friend

- her heart was shattered. Halle had no idea who to turn to - her best friend betrayed her. She was ashamed to vent on social media because of the perfect image she constructed for her relationship. The world believed things were great at home because that's the way Halle wanted them to see it. But now that the cracks in her glass house began to spread, she worried it was all going to fall apart.

After weeks of begging for forgiveness and heartfelt promises of a new and improved man, Halle made the unpopular decision to forgive Maurice and stay in her relationship.

For the first six months, the new Maurice was refreshing. He was much more attentive to her concerns and far more aware of her feelings. Halle, on the other hand, was a lesser version of herself. She was clearly not the same person. She smiled through her pain, but the security she once felt before was lost. The way she allowed love to flow through her was now being filtered through mistrust and doubt. He could no longer have the best Halle because that Halle was no longer there. The primary reason they remained together was Halle's fear that if she left him, her ex-best friend would have him.

The constant arguments in front of their child spread negative energy throughout the home. As time drifted on, Halle and Maurice knew things were coming to an end. The energy wasn't the same. Her effort in bed wasn't there, even though he was doing more than he had ever before.

Nine months after learning of Maurice's affair, he and Halle decided to call it quits. She told people they grew apart; he told people she was crazy.

What hurt the most was when she had to tell her six-year-old son that *daddy* wouldn't be around as much anymore. She worried that staying would prevent her from being the mother her son needed to thrive. However, she also feared that leaving and raising her son without a father in the home might be equally harmful. This wasn't the first time Maurice would play a lesser role in their child's life. Running the streets kept him in and out of jail, but it also kept their home furnished. The apartment they lived in was in Halle's name, so she remained, and he moved out.

He eventually moved in with her ex-best friend.

# Children in a Bad Environment

It's our responsibility to leave this world better than we found it, and one of the best ways to do that is by raising children with wisdom, not just material gifts. The lessons we teach and the love we show will shape how they think and behave for the rest of their lives.

A child's first example of communication between a man and a woman comes from watching their parents. This is why it's crucial to monitor what they see and hear - from the shows they watch to how their parents speak to and about each other. In front of a child, your words should carry calm and care. Telling your child *"Your daddy isn't worth shit"* damages more than just the father's image - it damages the child's self-image too. When you paint a negative picture of their parent and then tell them they look like that parent, you're unknowingly teaching them to see themselves the same way.

The same applies when a father says things like, *"Your mother is the reason we're in this mess."* Comments like that plant seeds of resentment that grow over time. Children shouldn't be dragged into adult conflicts. Some parents justify it by saying they're "keeping it real," but in reality, they're robbing their child of innocence. Protecting your child's mind means protecting their peace. Just because they'll eventually face adult problems doesn't mean they need to face them now. Childhood should be a time of learning, curiosity, and love - not emotional burden.

Venting to your child about your stress or your relationship isn't healthy. Your child is not your therapist. Energy doesn't disappear; it transfers. When you pour your negative energy into your child, you might feel lighter afterward, but they're now carrying what you released. You've taken something off your chest, but you've put it on theirs.

Parents sometimes say they're "preparing their child for the real world," but what they're really doing is introducing them to pain too early. I've seen parents teach toughness instead of wisdom - raising kids to fight through the streets rather than to avoid them altogether. There's a difference between preparing your child to survive and preparing them to thrive.

Teaching your child what to do when the lights are cut off is survival. Teaching them how to keep the lights on is wisdom. Many parents stop at survival. But our goal should be to help them build the kind of life where survival isn't their only option.

## **BOUNDARIES BETWEEN PARENTS**

Co-parenting has become common in today's world. While most people don't plan to be single parents, life happens - relationships end, and two people have to learn how to raise one child separately.

When a relationship ends, emotions can run high, but your child shouldn't feel that tension. You have to protect their peace while balancing your own pain. The love between two people may have faded, but the responsibility to raise a child remains. That's why setting boundaries and guidelines early on is so important.

If the relationship is truly over, stop trying to hold onto what's already broken by continuing to sleep together. Physical connection after a breakup can feel comforting, but it only confuses things. It gives the illusion of peace without solving the problem that caused the breakup. You can't let go of pain while holding on to pleasure from the same source. If it's done, let it be done.

When co-parenting, both sides need clear expectations. Talk about the basics:

- How much time the child will spend in each home
- What foods the child can and can't eat
- How much notice each parent needs for visits or pick-ups
- Who handles which financial responsibilities

These might seem simple, but without them, small issues can turn into big problems. If you're dealing with a man who refuses to set boundaries or discuss responsibilities, that can make things harder. Still, your focus should remain on your child's well-being.

Even if you and the father have different approaches, you both should want what's best for your child. You can't force him to see things your way, but you can set an example through your own actions. For instance, if you're against letting your child eat too much sugar but he's not, teach your child why too much candy isn't healthy. Show them videos or examples and ask their teacher to reinforce the lesson. That way, even when they're with their father, they'll understand why certain choices matter.

At the end of the day, do your part. You can't control the other parent or the world around your child, but you can control your own influence. Your consistency and love will stand out far more than the chaos that surrounds them.

## Incoming Incarceration

Sometimes the person you have a child with makes choices that risk their freedom. Other times, you knew exactly what kind of man he was before you got involved. Either way, a parent's decisions don't just affect them - they ripple into the lives of everyone connected, especially their children.

Not all crimes are equal, but the result of incarceration is often the same: absence. When a father ends up behind bars, it leaves a void in a child's life that can be hard to fill. A parent who can't keep themselves safe can't always protect their family. That's why judgment and self-control are so important in a parent.

A home should be a place of safety, where a child feels protected from the world. When a parent's actions threaten that security, adjustments must be made.

If the father is incarcerated, the mother is often forced to take on both roles - nurturer and disciplinarian. Over time, she becomes the child's main source of guidance and structure.

That's a heavy load to carry. Raising a child alone is one of the hardest things a person can do. For mothers raising sons, it's especially important to make sure positive male influences are present - uncles, cousins, brothers, or trusted family friends who can show him healthy examples of manhood. Boys need to see what responsible men look like.

This doesn't mean every man who shows interest in you should be allowed into your child's life. A new boyfriend, especially one you barely know, isn't a father figure. Your child doesn't need to meet a new man every few months. Let them build lasting bonds with people who are consistent and who care about them for real - not because of their relationship with you, but because of family or genuine love.

Having a partner in jail comes with emotional challenges, too. You may feel lonely, abandoned, or angry. If you've been through loss or trauma before, this situation can reopen old wounds. Some women stay, some leave immediately, and others struggle somewhere in between. Every situation is different.

Still, if you chose this lifestyle knowing the risks, it's only fair to accept what comes with it. Supporting him during the consequences of his choices is part of that commitment. But if you didn't sign up for this - if you were blindsided - then you have every right to reassess your situation. You didn't agree to this lifestyle, and you shouldn't feel obligated to live it.

What matters most is you and your child's well-being. If a man is behind bars, he should understand that your priority has to be raising that child in peace, stability, and love.

## **Prison Promises**

Be careful when it comes to prison promises. When a man's fast life suddenly stops, the silence of confinement can shock his mind. That pause gives him time to think - about his mistakes, his regrets, and the people he's lost. For some, that silence leads to real growth. But for others, it becomes a tool of manipulation.

When loneliness hits, many men reach out to the people who will keep them emotionally alive. Women - especially nurturing, loyal women - often become their main source of comfort. There's nothing wrong with offering support during hard times; love naturally wants to help.

The problem comes when he builds a fake sense of love just to keep your attention while he serves his time. It's not growth - it's survival.

A man behind bars knows that "out of sight, out of mind" is a real threat. So, he does everything he can to keep himself fresh in your heart. He'll call, write letters, or send messages promising a new beginning.

He'll swear things will be different when he gets out. He'll say things like:
- *"We're getting married when I come home."*
- *"When I get home, things will be different."*
- *"I've been reading and bettering myself."*
- *"This time, I'm staying out of trouble."*
- *"I found God."*
- *"It's all about family now."*

And sometimes, when he feels you slipping away, he'll even play reverse psychology:
- *"You can see other men if you want."*

That's just bait. It's meant to make you prove your loyalty by saying, *"No, I only want you."*

While some men mean every word, the real test starts when those prison gates open. Promises made in confinement sound perfect because temptation doesn't exist behind bars. It's the outside world that exposes what's real and what's not.

That's why you shouldn't dismiss everything he says - but you shouldn't believe it blindly either. Growth takes time, and words without action are just noise. If he truly wants to prove he's changed, he'll show it through consistency after release - not just with you, but with his life.

It's easy to find faith in a cage. The challenge is keeping it in freedom.

# **DEATH OF A PARENT**

Life can hit hard in ways we never expect. Losing a parent while trying to raise a child alone is one of those moments that shakes everything. Being a single parent is already tough - being the surviving parent of a child who's lost one of theirs is even harder.

I once had a young woman tell me she'd rather her son's father be dead, just so she'd know he didn't choose to walk away. I told her that how she feels doesn't matter as much as how the child would feel. A child might grow up with resentment or confusion after being abandoned, but death is final. There's no chance for redemption. No apology. No reconnection.

The truth is, even when parents separate, there's always the possibility for healing later in life. A father and child can still rebuild a bond when the time is right. My own relationship with my father didn't truly grow strong until I was thirty-five years old - and I'm thankful for that. So, just because the romantic chapter between you and the father is over doesn't mean his story with his child has to end too.

When it comes to explaining tragedy to a child, timing and language matter. Some parents speak too bluntly; others avoid the conversation altogether. I believe in following God's example - giving only as much truth as a child can handle, in a way that their heart can understand. You don't have to share every detail for them to grasp the loss.

It's okay to protect their innocence. Let them see the parent they lost as a symbol of strength, someone who loved them deeply. There's no harm in letting them hold on to that image.

I'd rather a child have a loving memory to comfort them than a harsh truth that steals their peace too soon.

We already live in a world where children are forced to grow up fast. Social media, television, and peer influence rush them into maturity before they're ready. Don't add to that. Let them be children for as long as they can.

———

In the end, as the comedian Chris Rock once said, *"You can drive a car with your feet if you want to - that doesn't make it a good idea."* You can raise a child alone, but that doesn't mean it's the best way. Still, when the other parent brings more harm than good, being alone might be the safer choice.

When tragedy strikes, do everything you can to shield your child from *your* personal stress. Let them laugh, play, and dream. Even without their father present, let their hero live on in the stories you tell and the love you continue to show.

## Read Halle's story again, what do you think she should do

# THE BOOK OF AVA

**OH! THE DISRESPECT**

Life grew increasingly challenging for Ava as Aiden's behavior took a bizarre turn. The emotional connection they once shared seemed to evaporate, leaving Ava feeling lost and disconnected. She couldn't shake the feeling that something was off, noticing the subtle shifts in Aiden's demeanor, his distant gaze, and lack of physical affection. The man who once adored her seemed like a stranger; his warm touch replaced by cold indifference. Ava was suffocating. Her best friend, Charity, seemed to be her rock during these troubling times. Charity frequently urged Ava to leave Aiden, insisting that he wasn't good for her. *"You deserve so much better,"* Charity would say, her eyes filled with concern. Despite Charity's constant warnings, Ava found it hard to let go of him, hoping things would return to the way they once were.

The turning point came on a rainy night when Ava's intuition screamed for answers she could no longer ignore. With trembling hands, she decided to investigate Aiden's phone. Her heart raced as she unlocked it, hoping to find nothing but fearing the worst. What she discovered shattered her world - Aiden had been engaging in malicious gossip, spreading lies about her to their social circle through text. Suddenly, friends whom she once trusted began to treat her differently, their doubtful glances amplifying her sense of isolation. Whispers followed her everywhere; each one a reminder of the lies Aiden had spun.

Adding insult to injury, Aiden's friends, sensing her vulnerability, attempted to insert themselves into Ava's life, further undermining her sense of security and trust. Their sly remarks and flirtatious advances only deepened Ava's wounds. It felt as if the walls were closing in, every familiar face now a potential threat.

Confronting Aiden about his actions brought little closure. Despite his apologies, which seemed hollow in the face of his deceit, Ava found herself standing alone, wounded by the betrayal of the one person she believed she could rely on.

Aiden's claims of wanting to be with her rang false, his actions consistently betraying his words. He made no genuine effort to win her back, his empty promises serving only to salt her wounds.

As Ava struggled to rebuild her shattered life, she found an unexpected ally in her best friend, Charity. Charity had been telling Ava for months to leave Aiden, insisting he wasn't good for her. Charity's constant warnings echoed in Ava's mind as she tried to make sense of the betrayal.

But one day, Ava stumbled upon a series of new texts on Charity's phone that revealed a sinister truth. Charity had not been looking out for Ava's best interests. Instead, she had been plotting to take Aiden for herself. Her seemingly protective advice was a manipulative tactic to drive a wedge between Ava and Aiden, ensuring that Aiden would eventually fall into her waiting arms.

The realization hit Ava like a freight train. Charity, the person she had confided in, the one she thought was her staunchest ally, had been betraying her all along. It wasn't just Aiden's betrayal that cut deep; it was Charity's deception that truly broke her. The friend she had trusted with her deepest fears and insecurities had been scheming behind her back, driven by selfish desires.

With a newfound strength, Ava confronted Charity. The confrontation was explosive, emotions running high as the truth spilled out. Charity, caught off guard, tried to justify her actions, but there was no justification that could mend the deep wounds she had inflicted.

In that moment, Ava realized she was better off without both Aiden and Charity. She walked away from the toxic entanglements that had suffocated her for so long. As she stepped into the night, she felt a weight lift off her shoulders. The scars would remain, but she was no longer defined by them. Ava was free, and for the first time in a long time, she could breathe.

## He Doesn't Find Me Sexy Anymore

It's natural to crave validation from the person you love. Everyone wants to feel wanted, admired, and desired. But sometimes, you can sense that your man no longer looks at you the same way he once did. That realization can hurt, but it doesn't always mean he's stopped loving you. Attraction is layered - it's built on emotion, curiosity, and consistency, not just looks.

### Communication Breakdowns

One of the biggest reasons attraction fades is silence. When couples stop communicating about what they like, want, or feel, distance grows without either person noticing. Early in a relationship, everything is exciting. You ask questions, share fantasies, and explore each other's needs. But over time, people start assuming the other already knows. They stop checking in. They stop talking about the things that keep love alive. When that happens, emotional closeness begins to slip, and physical intimacy follows.

If you feel this gap forming, talk. Not with attitude, not with blame - just talk. Tell him what you miss, what makes you feel alive, and what brings you closer. Listen when he shares his side.

Communication isn't about who's right; it's about reminding each other that you still care enough to try.

### Familiarity and Comfort

When you've been with someone for a while, the mystery fades. You know each other's routines, quirks, and habits. Familiarity can be comforting - but too much of it can kill excitement. That early spark was built on discovery. Once everything becomes predictable, curiosity disappears. Sometimes it's not that he doesn't find you sexy anymore - it's that he's forgotten how to see you.

Bring back surprise. Do something unexpected, wear something new, or plan a night that breaks routine. You don't have to reinvent yourself; just remind him that you're still the woman he fell for, only more seasoned, more confident, and more aware of what you bring to the table.

### External Stressors

Sometimes it has nothing to do with you. Work, bills, and responsibilities can drain a man's energy until he has nothing left to give emotionally or physically. Stress kills desire faster than time ever could. When his mind is heavy, affection becomes an afterthought. Don't take it personally - he might just be surviving the weight of his own worries. Ask him how he's really doing. Encourage him to breathe, rest, and reset. Sometimes love isn't about fixing him; it's about being a calm space for him to land.

### Evolving Together

You're not the same woman you were when he met you. Life has shaped you - new experiences, new confidence, new priorities. That's beautiful growth. But sometimes, change creates distance if both partners aren't evolving at the same pace. Independence is powerful, but a relationship still needs shared energy to thrive. Include him in your growth. Let him rediscover the new parts of you instead of feeling like he's lost the old ones. And if he's growing too, celebrate that instead of competing with it. Growth should be something you do together, not apart.

Your value doesn't shrink just because his attention has. Your beauty isn't defined by his eyes - it's reflected in how you see yourself. If you notice you've changed, embrace it. He might just need to catch up to the woman you've become.

## HE HAD SEX WITH MY BEST FRIEND

There are few betrayals deeper than being cheated on by the two people you trusted most. When your man crosses that line with

your best friend, it cuts differently.
It's not just heartbreak - it's humiliation mixed with confusion. You replay every moment, every conversation, wondering how long they've both been lying to you.

When a man cheats, it doesn't always mean he stopped loving you. Sometimes, it means he stopped respecting the relationship. He may tell himself it was just sex or a mistake, but the truth is, he disrespected the bond that was supposed to protect both of you. That's why, when you confront him, he might say, "But I love you." He's not lying about the love - he's just blind to what that love was supposed to require.

A man without discipline is a man without direction. Lust runs his life. He falls for every temptation that whispers his name. He'll promise himself it's just one time, but every time becomes another time. And once he's ruled by temptation, there's no limit to how low he might go.

When that lust pulls him toward someone close to you, the betrayal goes beyond the act - it's spiritual theft. He took something sacred that wasn't his to take. And if your friend accepted it, she participated in stealing your peace.

Still, ask yourself honestly - did you ever give him too much access to temptation? Did you ever overshare? Sometimes we unintentionally light fires we never meant to start. When you tell your man how wild your friend can be, or tell your friend how good your man is in bed, curiosity gets planted in both minds. It doesn't excuse them - but it explains how easily weak people fall.

So here's the takeaway: keep your private life private. Don't hand out information about your partner or your bedroom. Don't invite energy into your relationship that doesn't belong there. Protect your connection like you'd protect a child - because if it's valuable, it deserves to be guarded.

This kind of betrayal isn't about you being less than enough - it's about them being less than loyal.

## HE SAYS HE STILL WANTS ME... HE'S LYING

After a breakup, it's common for a man to suddenly say he wants you back. He'll call, text, or show up at your door with words that sound sincere. But more often than not, those words come from guilt, not growth.

He's not trying to rebuild what he broke - he's trying to rewrite how the story ends. Many men can't handle being the villain. They don't want to carry the blame or face what they did, so they try to end things on better terms. That's why he says, *"I still love you"* or *"I can change."* He's not necessarily lying about loving you - he's lying about being ready to do what that love requires.

Real change takes time. It takes self-reflection, not sweet talk. A man who truly understands his mistakes won't rush to get you back; he'll focus on fixing what made him lose you. The quick *"I'm sorry"* or *"I'll do better"* isn't growth - it's damage control. He's trying to make you stop crying, not trying to become the man you deserve.

Some men say they want you back because they can't stand the thought of someone else having you. The idea of another man holding what they lost bruises their ego. It's not always about love - it's about ownership. The thought of you finding peace, stability, and love with someone better highlights every flaw they refused to fix.

When he says, *"I've learned my lesson,"* pay attention to what he's actually learned. Did he learn to control his impulses? Did he learn discipline?

Or did he just learn what it takes to get you back temporarily?

A man who's truly changed will have proof in his actions. You won't have to ask him how he's different - you'll see it. You'll see discipline where there was carelessness. You'll see consistency where there was chaos.

So, if he can't explain what he's doing to manage his temptations, rebuild trust, or grow as a man - he's lying to you and to himself. Don't fall for the performance of remorse. Tears dry up, but habits remain.

If he hasn't changed the way he thinks, he hasn't changed the way he'll treat you.

## His Friends Are Now Hitting On Me

After a breakup, it can be confusing - and even disrespectful - when your ex's friends start showing interest in you. But this happens more often than people admit, and the reasons usually reveal more about them than they do about you.

Sometimes it starts with curiosity. If your ex talked about you to his friends - especially if he bragged about your looks, your personality, or even your sex life - they've already built a version of you in their heads. Once the relationship ends, those same friends may see an opening to make a move. They feel like they already "know" you, even though what they know came through him.

Other times, it's about ego. Some men want to prove they're just as good - or better - than their friend. Being with his ex feels like a trophy, something that raises their social status. It's not love; it's a competition. They want the story that says, *"I had her too."* It's the same type of validation people chase when they brag about sleeping with someone famous or popular.

In some cases, your ex's friends saw how he mistreated you and thought they could do better. They watched him take you for granted, and now they want to step in, either because they genuinely liked you all along or because they see a chance to "win" where he failed. But even if their intentions seem good, crossing that line usually shows a lack of respect for boundaries and loyalty.

And then there's the quiet truth - some of them were always attracted to you. They just waited for the relationship to end so they could make their move without looking disloyal. But their patience doesn't make it right.

Whatever their reason, one thing stays the same: when a man's friends hit on you, it says more about their lack of integrity than it does about your attractiveness. The best thing you can do is protect your peace. Recognize the pattern and know that if they could betray their friend's trust that easily, they'll do the same to you.

## THE GOSSIP KING

There are few things more disappointing than a man who gossips about his woman. Whether he's exposing private details, exaggerating the truth, or flat-out lying, it shows weakness and immaturity. Real men protect their woman's name - they don't drag it through conversations for attention or pity.

When a man speaks badly about his woman to others, it usually means he doesn't see her as his closest confidant. Instead of building a safe space for the two of them to share their problems, he takes his issues outside the relationship, looking for validation from friends, coworkers, or even social media. That's a dangerous habit because once outsiders are involved, they form opinions and take sides. What should've stayed between two people becomes a community discussion.

In healthy relationships, your partner should be your home - the one person you can talk to about anything. Even when things go wrong, your loyalty should keep their image protected. A man who truly loves and respects his woman doesn't allow others to speak badly about her, and he certainly doesn't contribute to it.

When a relationship has a deep connection, how your partner is seen by others matters. You don't need to live your life for the approval of others, but your reputation and how you present your partner reflect your character. The world should see the love you have for each other, not hear about your private arguments or her flaws.

When a man tarnishes his woman's image, it says more about him than her. It shows his insecurities and lack of self-control. A real man uplifts his woman in public and corrects her in private, not the other way around.

So if your man spends more time talking about you than talking to you, take note. He may not realize it, but he's revealing his immaturity and insecurity every time your name leaves his mouth in the wrong tone.

Protecting your woman's reputation is part of being her man. Her name should be safe in every room you enter. Because if you truly value her, you won't let gossip be the thing that breaks what love built.

## Read Ava's story again, what do you think she should do

# THE BOOK OF
# LESLIE

**HOW GOOD IN BED IS HE REALLY**

Leslie, at 32, found herself increasingly disheartened by her sex life with Jon. Each sexual encounter had become a dull routine, stripping away any traces of passion. She longed for a connection that went beyond the ordinary, yet Jon's mechanical and uncaring approach only deepened her sense of isolation. His routine questions about her satisfaction felt more like checkpoints than expressions of genuine care. The words, *"Did you cum?"* linger painfully in her memories.

The lack of enthusiasm during oral sex further compounded Leslie's frustration. It wasn't just about the physical act; it was the yearning for a bond that reached beyond the surface. The bedroom, once a haven of closeness, had turned into a piercing reminder of unmet needs and unspoken disappointments.

Leslie's emotions became a tangled web of confusion and self-doubt. She questioned whether her dissatisfaction stemmed from poor choices in partners or something inherently wrong within herself. This internal conflict gnawed at her, leading to guilt-ridden thoughts of ending the relationship solely due to bad sex.

In her quiet moments, Leslie began a journey of *self-reflection*. She sought to understand if she truly deserved a love that was both passionate and understanding. The routine of their encounters served as a mirror, reflecting the harsh reality of her choices. She stood at a crossroads, faced with the painful decision of settling for less or daring to pursue the kind of intimacy she deeply craved. As her inward searching deepened, she came to a sobering realization: perhaps, her experiences were shaped not just by the men she chose, but by her own evolving understanding of what she truly needed. She was learning herself and within that, she realized the things that stimulated her before were maybe no more.

## THE CAN AND WANT THEORY

Many single women say they don't feel a deep connection during sex, even when they're in a relationship. The reason often ties back to what I call *The Can and Want Theory*. It explains why so many women end up physically unsatisfied - because some men are with women they can have, not women they truly want.

When a man doesn't have to work hard to get a woman, he usually puts in less effort in bed. That's because she wanted him more than he wanted her. There's no chase, no real excitement, no emotional fire behind the act. So the experience becomes one-sided.

Most women, on the other hand, are more selective about who they sleep with. They tend to choose men they genuinely desire, which makes their intimacy more passionate and personal. Even if the sex isn't perfect, it feels deeper because she's emotionally invested.

Men often choose the easier option - the woman who's available, not necessarily the one they desire. They feel comfortable dating or sleeping with women who match or fall below their level, while women usually reach for partners who match or rise above them. Because of this, a lot of men end up in sexual situations with women they're not even attracted to beyond the physical act itself.

When he doesn't feel a true spark, his effort shows it. He's not driven to impress her or please her. And when the connection isn't mutual, the sex usually isn't satisfying for her either.

Society adds to the problem. Women are taught to look for emotional connection and long-term compatibility, while men are often encouraged to chase convenience and opportunity. That difference in motivation is why so many women feel a disconnect during intimacy - they're looking for meaning while he's looking for a moment.

So if he's not putting effort into pleasing you, it could be because he doesn't see you as his equal. Maybe you were just the most available option when he wanted company. But that's not on you - that's his lack of depth and self-control. When people settle, they stop trying. They don't nurture what they have because, deep down, they never valued it fully in the first place.

*The Can and Want Theory* reminds us that desire matters. It's not about ego or playing hard to get - it's about knowing that mutual interest fuels passion. Don't settle for someone who simply can have you. Wait for the one who truly wants you. If he thinks you're replaceable, let him replace you. All that does is make space for the man who will value you completely.

## LISTEN TO HER BODY

A lot of men learn about sex the wrong way - from porn. They watch scenes that are staged for the camera and assume that's what women really want. They confuse performance with passion. They think fast, aggressive, or forceful means satisfying, not realizing most of that is acting. What works in a film doesn't always work in real life.

A man should move like water - smooth, adaptable, and in rhythm with his partner. When a woman's body shifts, tenses, or softens, she's speaking without words. If he ignores that language, he's just forcing his way down a path that was meant to be shared. Sure, he might reach the end, but neither of them will enjoy the journey.

Too many men use the same sexual routine with every woman, thinking one formula fits all. It doesn't. Every woman has her own rhythm, pace, and needs. The best lovers are students of the body - they pay attention, learn, and adjust. Listening to her body is how a man learns to please her.

The problem is that many men separate intimacy from sex. They see the act as a goal rather than an exchange. For them, sex becomes about release, not connection. Intimacy is optional, not necessary. But for most women, sex without intimacy feels empty - it's physical but not emotional.

If he doesn't truly care about you, that detachment will show in bed. A man who's only focused on himself will move like someone racing against a clock, not someone trying to share an experience. Pleasing you requires selflessness, and selfish men rarely have that quality.

It's also worth noting how your attitude before sex shapes the moment. If he senses that you're only doing it because he wants to, he may not put in much effort. If you respond with an unenthusiastic *"Fine, but make it quick,"* he'll probably treat the moment like a chore. When you act like you don't want it, he acts like you don't deserve it.

The body doesn't lie. A man who truly listens - to your sounds, your breathing, your movements - learns you better than any words could teach him. That's real intimacy. It's not just about what happens in bed - it's about learning to connect, not perform.

## EMOTIONAL INTIMACY

True connection goes deeper than the physical. Emotional intimacy is what keeps a relationship alive when the spark fades. It's the comfort of knowing someone sees you, understands you, and still chooses you. Without that emotional bond, sex eventually feels hollow, and conversations start sounding routine.

Emotional intimacy starts with communication. Not just talking, but actually being honest and vulnerable. It's about saying what's really on your mind without worrying about being judged. When both partners can do that, it builds trust. And once trust grows, love feels safer to express.

Listening is another piece of it. Too often, people hear words but don't listen to feelings. Real listening means noticing the pauses, the tone, and the emotion behind the words.

When someone feels truly heard, walls come down. That's when closeness begins.

Vulnerability is the bridge between two hearts. Letting your guard down is hard, but it's also how love deepens. Emotional intimacy can't exist where fear and pride live. When both people are willing to show their weaknesses and share their pain, the relationship becomes stronger.

Shared experiences matter too. Whether it's traveling, laughing over dinner, or just surviving a tough day together, those moments form emotional glue. They remind you both that you're a team, not two individuals competing for control.

Empathy is another key. It means feeling what your partner feels, not just observing it. When you understand their emotions as if they were your own, you create a connection that no argument can easily break.

Emotional intimacy doesn't build itself. It's an ongoing process, something both people have to work at. That might mean checking in with each other, being open about stress, or simply saying *"I love you"* without reason.

When emotional intimacy is strong, sex naturally becomes better. Because when two people are emotionally connected, the bedroom isn't just about pleasure - it's about passion and peace. The more you understand someone's life, the deeper you'll care. And the deeper you care, the stronger the bond becomes - inside and outside the sheets.

## UNMET PHYSICAL DESIRES

Sometimes sex feels one-sided - not because there's no attraction, but because someone isn't being heard. Many women feel unseen in bed, and often it comes down to one thing: communication.

If you don't talk about what feels good and what doesn't, he'll assume everything's fine. Most men aren't mind readers; they go off reaction, not intuition. That's why it's so important to speak up - but how you say it matters just as much as what you say.

For example, instead of saying, *"I don't like when you go so fast inside me,"* try saying, *"Bae, it felt sooo good when you started going slow inside me. I like that part best."* The first statement feels like a critique; the second feels like an invitation.

One builds resistance, the other builds connection.

Society puts pressure on men to "perform," to live up to certain standards. That mindset can sometimes make sex feel like a test instead of an experience. When a man is focused on proving something, he stops focusing on you. Helping him let go of that pressure - by reassuring him that sex is about connection, not performance - can make a huge difference.

Some men also lack knowledge about a woman's body. They may not fully understand what creates real pleasure. This isn't always about ego - it's often about inexperience or misinformation. A woman's anatomy and arousal process require patience and awareness, not assumption. Watching an educational video together or simply exploring at a slower pace can help both of you learn each other's rhythm without judgment.

Insecurity also plays a big role. If a man struggles with performance issues, his mind becomes his biggest enemy. He focuses on lasting instead of connecting, and that pressure kills the mood. He needs reassurance, not ridicule. A safe, supportive response helps rebuild his confidence so he can relax and be present.

Sex should be teamwork. Both people should walk away feeling seen, satisfied, and connected. If one person walks away empty, something's missing. Communication and *gentleness* - not demands or blame can bring the balance back.

As my grandmother used to tell my girl cousins, *"You catch more flies with honey than with vinegar."*

## Downtown

Oral sex, when done right, can take things to another level. It's one of the most intimate, ego-free ways two people can connect. But a lot of women go through life never really being pleased that way - and some start thinking maybe it's just not for them. The truth is, the problem isn't them. It's usually him.

Let's be real. Some men won't go down there, and most won't admit why. For a lot of them, it's ego or immaturity. They'll brag about what they can do in bed, but avoid the part that requires selflessness. Sex to them is about dominance, not connection. But going down takes humility - it's about giving, not taking.

There are a few common reasons he may not be doing it.

1. **Looks.** Some men will sleep with a woman they find decent but won't put their face between her legs. That's just the truth. They might find her attractive enough to have sex with but not enough to be fully intimate. They think oral sex is something you do for the woman you really want, not the woman you're just sleeping with. It's shallow thinking, but it's real.

2. **Cleanliness.** Hygiene matters for both people. If he smells bad, you're not going to want his face near you either. But for some men, even the slightest odor - real or imagined - turns them off. So they'll skip it completely. There are men who've literally hit it from behind while holding their breath. Nobody wants to say that out loud, but it's true. Intercourse is given more grace than oral sex. Good hygiene can make a big difference in some cases. Making sure you shower right before sex can be the game changer for some.

3. **Lack of experience.** Some men were never taught how to please a woman beyond penetration. Maybe past partners didn't care much for it or never corrected them.

Maybe they tried it once, didn't get the reaction they expected, and never tried again. Whatever the reason, it's often not about not wanting to - it's about not knowing how or being too prideful to ask.

And lastly, past trauma or mental blocks. If a man was ever shamed or had a bad experience, he might associate oral with discomfort or disgust. That takes time and patience to overcome. But he has to be willing to talk about it, because you can't fix what he hides.

Older men, though - they know better. When age humbles you, you stop worrying about what makes you look powerful and start focusing on what makes her feel good. Some even find peace in it. Even if their penis doesn't perform like it used to, their tongue can still do the job, and they take pride in that.

Oral sex is just another form of communication. It's a way of saying, *"I want you to feel good."* If he refuses to speak that language, it's not just about what he won't do - it's about what he doesn't understand. You deserve a man who's fluent in *you*.

## ANTI-TOY

Some men see toys as the enemy. The minute you pull one out, they feel challenged, like you're saying their penis isn't enough. They start taking it personal instead of realizing it's just an enhancement, not a replacement.

For a lot of guys, sex is tied to ego. They don't make love to connect; they make love to prove something. Every stroke is about dominance, not pleasure. So when you bring a toy into that space, it messes with their image of control. Suddenly, it's not just him making you moan - it's a device. And that bruises the ego.

But the truth is, toys can change the entire game. They can take what's good and make it unforgettable. They can fill in the gaps that his body can't always handle - whether it's endurance, size, or stamina. It's not about saying he's less of a man; it's about saying you want more of the experience.

A confident man won't see that as a threat. He'll use it as a tool. He'll learn how your body reacts and work with it instead of against it. The insecure man, though, will retreat. He'll make excuses, joke about it, or say, *"You don't need that if you got me."* That's not confidence, that's insecurity dressed up as pride.

If his body isn't performing how it used to, toys can take the pressure off. They can help him please you while he gets his own rhythm back. But most men never get that far because they'd rather protect their ego than protect your pleasure.

A man who's truly connected to you will understand that pleasing you is the ultimate power move. It's not about who or what gets you there - it's about the fact that he made sure you did.

Real men don't compete with toys. They hold them. They use them. They learn from them. And when it's all said and done, they still make you call out their name.

## Sexual Intelligence

Sexual intelligence isn't just about knowing how to make someone cum. It's about knowing how to connect. It's understanding what turns your partner on mentally, emotionally, and physically - and being aware enough to notice the small details that most people miss.

It's not just about technique; it's about awareness. Sexual intelligence starts with knowing yourself - your limits, your triggers, your desires. Most people skip that part.

They learn what looks good in porn or what someone else liked once, and they try to copy it. But real intimacy doesn't come from imitation; it comes from communication.

A man who's sexually intelligent listens - not just with his ears, but with his hands, his eyes, and his timing. He notices the small changes in your breath, the twitch in your thigh, the sound you make when he's hitting the right spot. He reads your body like a language, and every movement becomes a sentence.

Empathy plays a huge role in this. You have to care enough to understand how your partner feels, not just what they like. You can't fake that. When you care, you adjust. You slow down. You pay attention. You want them to feel good, not just to say you did a good job.

Being sexually intelligent also means being curious. Try new things. Talk about fantasies. Ask questions that matter - "What turns you on?" shouldn't be an interview question; it should be an ongoing conversation. Growth doesn't stop once you've had great sex.

The more you explore together, the deeper your connection becomes.

And that's the point - connection. Sex without connection is just friction. But when both people bring emotional intelligence into it, when they're open, curious, and aware, it becomes something spiritual. Something that lingers. Something that makes you crave the person even when they're not around.

You don't need to be a genius to have sexual intelligence. You just need to pay attention - and give a damn.

## Managing Body Insecurities in Intimate Moments

A lot of women struggle with body insecurities that creep into the bedroom and ruin the moment before it even starts. Society has convinced too many women that they need to look perfect to be desired, but real men don't need perfection - they need connection.

If he's already hard, that tells you everything you need to know. He's turned on by you. Not the version of you that you wish existed, not the filtered picture in your phone, but the woman standing in front of him. If he didn't want you, his body wouldn't react the way it does.

When you're in bed with a man, be present. The quickest way to block your orgasm is to start worrying about your stomach, your thighs, or the sound you just made. Men are visual, yes, but they're also turned on by confidence. There's nothing sexier than a woman who moves like she owns her pleasure.

You might think your stretch marks, your tummy rolls, or your sagging breasts are a turn-off - but trust me, most men couldn't care less. They're too focused on how you make them feel. The way you moan, the way you grab them, the way you melt - those are the things that stay in their mind long after the lights go off.

I've heard women say, *"Men will fuck anything,"* and then turn around and feel insecure about their body during sex. You can't have it both ways. If men will sleep with anything, then clearly they don't care about your so-called imperfections. What matters is your energy - the vibe you bring to the room.

The truth is, what turns a man on more than how you look is how nasty you get. Confidence in bed trumps every insecurity you could ever imagine. If you want to wear your shirt, fine. If you want to take it off, even better. But don't do it because you think you're supposed to-do it because you want to.

When you let go of self-judgment and focus on pleasure, everything changes. You stop performing and start feeling. That's when the real orgasms come. That's when you stop having sex and start connecting.

It's okay to take that shirt off, sweetheart.

## The Guilt Trip

It's normal to feel guilty for wanting to leave a relationship just because the sex isn't good. But let's be honest - bad sex can slowly kill a relationship. Physical connection matters. It's not the only thing, but it's a major thing. When you start dreading intimacy or pretending to be satisfied, that guilt you feel isn't love - it's obligation.

Still, you have to remember your worth extends beyond what happens in the bedroom. A relationship is built on emotional, mental, and physical balance. When one of those pillars crumbles, it puts strain on the others.

Before walking away, though, you owe it to yourself to try fixing it the right way.

Start with appreciation. Tell him what you do like about him first. Set a positive tone so he doesn't shut down. Then move into the problem. Be specific. Don't say, *"The sex just sucks."* Instead, say, *"Lately I feel like we're not connecting in bed the way we used to."* That's an invitation, not an attack.

Express how it makes you feel. Use "I" statements, not "you" statements. *"I feel disconnected"* hits differently than *"You don't satisfy me."* It's all in the delivery. You want progress, not pride wars.

Then talk about your needs. Tell him what excites you, what you'd like to try. Encourage him to share his thoughts too. You'd be surprised how many men also feel disconnected but are too afraid to say it first. This is where you both can rebuild the spark - together.

Ask for his perspective. Let him talk. Even if what he says stings a bit, at least you'll know where his head is. Some men feel pressure to perform, others feel rejected when they sense your frustration. This honesty is how healing starts.

Explore solutions together. Try new things. Switch up positions, locations, routines. You don't have to turn into a porn star - just show interest. Bring back curiosity.

Maybe it's role-play, maybe it's toys, maybe it's simply slowing down and looking each other in the eyes again.

Set boundaries too. Talk about what's off limits and what's not. Make it safe to experiment. And have regular check-ins - not just when things go bad, but even when they're going great. "That last time was crazy… what did you like most about it?" Simple questions like that keep communication open.

But also be prepared for the truth. Sometimes, no matter how hard you try, he won't meet you halfway. That's when you have to decide what's best for you. If you've given your best and he's not trying, it might be time to reevaluate. You can't keep setting yourself on fire to keep someone else warm.

Nothing should keep a woman from having the orgasm she deserves.

## Read Leslie's story again, what do you think she should do?

# THE BOOK OF
# SARAH

**THE UNEXPECTED PROTECTOR**

Sarah never imagined herself in this situation, standing between two men who both claimed a place in her son's life. One was his biological father, Mark, and the other, her husband, Steve. The tension between them had been brewing for months, and today it finally reached a boiling point.

Sarah met Steve a year after she and Mark separated. Mark had been a part of her life since high school, but as they grew older, their paths diverged. He was a good father when he was around, but his visits became sporadic, and his interest waned. When

Steve came into their lives, he brought a sense of stability Sarah hadn't realized they were missing. From the beginning, Steve showed an unwavering commitment to both Sarah and her son, Jake. He attended school events, helped with homework, and played catch in the backyard. Jake adored him, calling him *"Dad"* more often than not, something that didn't sit well with Mark.

The incident happened on a Saturday at Jake's little league game. Steve was coaching the team, having volunteered at the start of the season. Mark showed up unexpectedly, his presence alone enough to make the air thick with unspoken words.

As the game ended, Jake ran to Steve, excitement lighting up his face. *"Did you see my catch, Dad?"* he beamed. Steve knelt down, ruffling Jake's hair. *"You were amazing out there, buddy. I'm so proud of you."*

Mark, standing a few feet away, stiffened. Sarah saw the storm brewing in his eyes. He walked over, a forced smile on his face. *"Great game, champ,"* he said, trying to reclaim his role. Jake looked between the two men, the confusion evident on his face.

"Jake, go get your things," Sarah said, trying to diffuse the situation. As he ran off, Mark turned to Steve. *"You know, it's confusing for him to call you 'Dad.' I'm his father."*

Steve stood up, his calm demeanor unwavering. *"I'm not trying to replace you, Mark. I'm here to support Jake and be there for him."*

The words were meant to be reassuring, but Mark took them as a challenge. *"Support him? By coaching his team? By letting him call you 'Dad'? You think you can just step in and take over?"*

Sarah stepped forward, placing a hand on Steve's arm, but he gently moved it away. *"I'm here because I love him, and I love Sarah. We're a family now."*

Mark's face reddened, his fists clenching. *"You have no idea what it means to be his father."*

Steve's voice remained steady, but there was a steel edge to it now. *"Maybe not, but I know what it means to be there for him."*

The tension was palpable, and for a moment, Sarah feared a physical confrontation. But then Jake reappeared, his eyes wide with worry. *"Mom, what's going on?"*

Both men turned to him, their expressions softening. *"Nothing, sweetheart,"* Sarah said quickly. *"Let's go home."*

Mark looked at Jake, then back at Steve, his anger slowly dissipating. *"We'll talk about this later,"* he muttered before walking away.

As they drove home, Jake sat quietly in the back seat, sensing the unease. Steve reached over and took Sarah's hand, his grip reassuring. *"I'm sorry,"* he said softly. *"I didn't mean to cause trouble."*

Sarah squeezed his hand back, grateful for his presence. *"You didn't. You're just being the man Jake needs."*

But as she said the words, doubt began to creep in. Was Steve really what Jake needed? Or was he just a convenient replacement for Mark? Would Jake grow up confused about who he felt his real father was?

That night, as she lay in bed, Sarah couldn't shake the feeling of uncertainty. She knew Steve loved Jake, but how much of this was driven by his desire to be a father and how much by his love for her? And what about Mark? Would he ever step up and be the father Jake needed?

The questions swirled in her mind, leaving her with a nagging sense of unease. She wanted to believe that everything would work out, but for now, she was left wondering what the future held for her, Steve, and Jake.... and mark.

## **THE STEPFATHER**

When a relationship ends and another begins, it's never just two people starting over. Children, memories, and lessons all come with you. Every new beginning comes with someone's past.

A man entering a relationship with real intentions knows that. He understands that if you have children, he's not just dating you - he's stepping into a family. But not every man carries that mindset. Some approach it lightly, seeing the child as an accessory rather than a responsibility. Others, men who are intentional, see it as his duty.

Many stepfathers take pride in their role. They love the idea of teaching, providing, and being the steady hand a child can depend on. Their love for their woman fuels their desire to help raise her child, and over time, that care becomes genuine love for the child too.

Then there are the ones who do the bare minimum. They hover in the background, only helping when told, never forming a bond, never trying to connect. They play the part of a man but lack the heart of a father.

Being a stepfather isn't about replacing anyone. It's about showing up, consistently, with patience and respect - for the woman and for her child.

# THE 2ND DAD

When the biological parents are co-parenting, the stepfather's role is different from when the biological father isn't in the picture. In this case, the stepfather becomes more of a second dad. His main focus is on how the child interacts with him, his woman, and the home they share. While he cares deeply for the child, his parenting is limited because the biological father is still involved and aware of what's happening in the child's life.

### Understanding the Role of the 2nd Dad

The stepfather's main job is to provide emotional support and stability within his household. He naturally cares for the child, but most of what he does supports the efforts of the biological father. Think of him as the Robin to the biological father's Batman.

He must also respect boundaries. Knowing where his role begins and ends is crucial. That means recognizing the father's authority and making sure his decisions never cross into another man's territory.

The second dad focuses on building a positive, genuine relationship with the child - one based on trust, understanding, and love. He learns the child's interests, shows up, and creates a bond that adds to the child's emotional development.

He also works to keep peace in the home. That means balancing his relationship with his partner, the child, and even the child's father. The goal is to build a home that feels calm, stable, and supportive.

## Dads Not Around

A stepfather thrives when he's given full authority to be a real father figure. That doesn't just mean handling discipline - it includes being part of every major decision about the child's life, like school, health, and daily routines.

When he's recognized as an important and trusted figure, he can give the child the type of stability and guidance that builds mutual respect and love. Without another man challenging his position, he's able to fully step into the role with confidence and care.

When a stepfather is truly integrated into the family, he becomes a vital part of the child's world. No one second-guesses his choices, and he can act with clarity and purpose, knowing he's trusted to do what's best. That confidence builds security for everyone in the household.

As he consistently shows up - helping with school, giving advice, being present - the child begins to see him as more than "mom's boyfriend." He becomes a true father figure. Often, that bond becomes so natural that the child starts calling him "Dad," and he proudly calls the child his son or daughter in return.

This bond can form even when the biological father is still alive, but it usually happens faster and deeper when the biological father isn't around. Without that competing presence, the family dynamic is simpler. The stepfather's role becomes clear, and the connection grows without confusion or conflict.

Still, even if the biological father is in the picture, a good stepfather can create a strong, positive bond by cooperating instead of competing. When both men put the child first, the result can be a healthy, balanced family structure where love and guidance come from multiple directions.

## IF IT WASN'T FOR YOUR MOTHER

When you bring a new man into your child's life, it's important to pay attention to his true intentions. Does he genuinely care about your child's well-being, or is he using your child to win you over? Some men will play the part of a loving father because they know it's the fastest way to your heart. They recognize that, as a mother, your instinct is to protect and provide for your children - and they use that to make you feel secure.

But sometimes, it's just an act. Behind the gestures and smiles, some of these men are living double lives. Their hearts and minds are never truly committed to the family they're pretending to build. They're physically present but emotionally absent.

Their motives vary - some need a place to stay, some crave the image of being a "family man," and others may even have another family elsewhere. No matter the reason, their actions eventually reveal the truth.

Here are *three red flags* to look out for:

## 1. Inconsistent Involvement

A man who only interacts with your child when it's convenient or when people are watching is not sincere. If his attention comes and goes - one day warm and loving, the next cold and detached - it's a clear sign he's performing, not parenting.

## 2. Lack of Initiative

A real father figure steps up without being told. If he never volunteers to help with homework, avoids school events, or waits for you to take the lead on everything, he's not invested. True care shows through consistent effort, not empty words.

## 3. Overemphasis on Appearance

Some men care more about looking like a good father than being one. They're affectionate in public or post sweet moments on social media, but at home, they're distant. The gestures are for show, not substance.

If he already has children, pay attention to how he treats them. A man's history is often the best indicator of his future behavior. People can grow, but patterns tell stories - and they're worth listening to.

## LISTEN TO YOUR CHILD

This world can be dangerous, and too many children suffer in silence because no one believed them. There have been far too many cases where a stepfather took advantage of a child's innocence - and it often started with the mother ignoring small signs. Always listen to your children.

When you bring a new man into your home, remember - your happiness matters, but your child's safety comes first. Love can make you overlook things, but never ignore your child's discomfort. If your child tells you something feels wrong, believe them. Even if you don't see it right away, investigate it.

Here are *six warning signs* to stay aware of:

1. **Excessive Alone Time**
If he's always trying to be alone with your child without a real reason - or gets defensive when questioned - that's a problem. A man with good intentions will never need privacy with your child.

2. **Overstepping Boundaries**
Any touching that makes your child uncomfortable, even small

gestures, should be taken seriously. If he ignores personal space or finds reasons to touch unnecessarily, don't brush it off.

### 3. Behavioral Changes in Your Child

Pay attention if your child suddenly becomes quiet, fearful, or withdrawn around him. If they start avoiding home or certain rooms, that's your cue to pay attention. Children often express fear through behavior before they find the words to explain it.

### 4. Excessive Control

If he monitors your child's activities too closely or insists on knowing everything they do and who they talk to, that's not protection - it's possession.

### 5. Inappropriate Conversations

If he starts talking about sex or private topics with your child - or tells them to keep "secrets" - take immediate action. That's a clear violation.

### 6. Unusual Attention and Gifts

Gifts can be sweet, but overdoing it can be a strategy. When gifts come with expectations or secrecy, be alert. Many predators start by creating comfort and joy before crossing lines.

It's important to understand - tragedy often hides behind what looks like kindness. Don't assume good behavior means good intentions. When a child says, "He's a bad man," don't immediately replay all the good things he's done to convince yourself otherwise. Children don't make up fear - they feel it.

Pay attention. Watch. Protect. Because once trust is broken in a child, it's almost impossible to fully restore.

## THE BIOLOGICAL FATHER

It's easy to dismiss the biological father and say, *"If he cared, he'd be here."* But whether you like him or not, he's still part of your child's DNA. That means your child will always have a connection to him - whether through curiosity, resentment, or longing. Even if your child agrees with you now, their perspective may change as they grow. So, his presence - or absence - still matters.

When talking about biological fathers, there are usually two kinds: the Bio-Hazard Dad and the Bio-Logical Dad.

## The Bio-Hazard Dad

Some fathers can't handle seeing you move on. When they see you happy, they start acting out, trying to cause chaos in your home just to prove they still have control. They might talk badly about your new man, interfere with your relationship, or try to scare him off.

This behavior isn't about love - it's about ego. These men feel powerless, and starting conflict gives them a sense of control. The problem is, their behavior doesn't just affect you; it affects your child.

When a father starts fights or shows up ready to argue, remember - boys fight to solve problems, men talk to solve problems. If your new man chooses violence or quick temper over conversation, that's another red flag. You're not just choosing a partner; you're choosing the environment your child grows up in.

Some men, when they were the ones who messed up the relationship, can't stand to see you at peace. They believe you should "pay" for what you did. Instead of focusing on being a father, they turn into the punishment. When that happens, the best thing you can do is protect you and your child's peace.

## The Bio-Logical Dad

Then you have the fathers who understand their role and handle it with maturity. They focus on being good dads - not ex-boyfriends. They communicate only about their child, stay in their lane, and respect your household as much as they expect you to respect theirs.

They may not care for your new partner, but as long as your child is safe and happy, they don't cause problems. They'll answer the phone when needed, show up when it matters, and stay consistent in their responsibilities. These men make co-parenting easier.

Then there are the assertive biological fathers. They're involved in every part of their child's life - family events, birthdays, school functions. They want to stay close, not out of jealousy, but because they care. Sometimes, they'll invite you and your new partner along to show inclusion, or maybe just to see how the dynamic works. It's partly genuine and partly protective.

Even though it can feel like they're doing too much, their intentions are usually centered on their child's well-being.

These fathers might be overbearing at times, but their goal is often to stay connected, not to stir up drama.

Whether he's the calm, mature type or the complicated one, your job is to manage the situation in a way that keeps your child safe and emotionally grounded. The biological father's energy will always affect the child - so the less chaos, the better.

## **FATHERS**

In the end, a good stepfather can be a blessing. When he embraces the role with love and consistency, he becomes more than a man in the home - he becomes a steady hand shaping a child's life. But the role isn't easy, especially if he has children of his own. That balance can weigh heavy. Sometimes, the mother of his biological child may resent his new commitment to your child, causing tension and even keeping his child away. Those emotional crossfires are real, and they can test even the strongest man.

For men who've never had children, becoming a stepfather can feel like a new purpose. It gives them a chance to nurture, guide, and experience the love of fatherhood - without the journey of childbirth.

And for men who can't have children of their own, it can feel like grace - a second chance to pour love into a young life and build something that lasts.

For women choosing a stepfather for their child, the decision goes beyond looks, charm, or income.

The real question is: Would I be proud if my son grew up to be like him? Your child will learn from his example - how he handles stress, how he speaks to you, how he moves through life. Choose a man who teaches strength through peace, not fear.

Fatherhood is more than a title - it's an assignment from God. Some waste it. Others rise to meet it. Real fathers understand that they're shaping not just a child, but the future. Their patience, their words, and their presence ripple through generations.

To the men who step up, who give love without limits, and who protect what's not biologically theirs but becomes theirs through care - you're the quiet heroes. The world may not praise you enough, but your legacy will live through the children who watched you love right.

And to the men who know they're not ready, that's okay too. Awareness is the first step to growth. Take that time to become the man your future family can count on.

Because true fatherhood isn't just raising a child - it's raising the standard.

## Read Sarah's story again, what do you think she's dealing with?

# THE BOOK OF
# MARY

**LOVE'S FINAL JOURNEY**

Mary and Willard had been married for 45 years, a union that had weathered the storms of life and emerged stronger. Their love story was one of companionship, shared dreams, and countless cherished moments. They had built a life together, raising children, celebrating milestones, and supporting each other through thick and thin.

One afternoon, they visited the hospital for what they thought would be a routine check-up. The atmosphere in the waiting room was filled with the soft hum of conversations and the occasional clinking of medical instruments. Mary held Willard's hand tightly, her thumb gently caressing his knuckles in a reassuring gesture. Despite the ordinary setting, an unspoken tension lingered in the air.

When the doctor finally called them in, they exchanged a hopeful glance before following him into a small, sterile room. The doctor's face was serious, and Mary's heart began to race. She felt a tightening in her chest as he began to speak, his words carefully measured but heavy with significance.

"Willard, I'm afraid we have some difficult news. The tests show that you have cancer."

The words hit Mary like a bolt of lightning, shattering the peaceful existence they had known. She watched as Willard's face went cold, his eyes wide with shock and fear. The lost look in his gaze mirrored the turmoil now raging inside of her. Mary, who had always been a pillar of strength, felt a wave of vulnerability wash over her. She reached for Willard's hand, gripping it as if to anchor them both against the storm that had suddenly engulfed their lives.

The drive home was silent, each of them lost in their own thoughts. Mary's mind raced through memories of their life together - the laughter, tears, the quiet moments of simple joy. How had they gone from those cherished times to this heartbreaking reality? She glanced at Willard, who stared blankly out the window, his usual calm demeanor replaced by a noticeable sense of despair.

At home, Mary busied herself with making tea, her hands trembling as she set the kettle on the stove. Willard sat at the kitchen table, his head in his hands. The sight of him so broken, so lost, made her heart ache. She wanted to say something, to comfort him, but words failed her.

As the days passed, the reality of their situation began to sink in. Willard's health began to deteriorate, and Mary found herself thrust into the role of caregiver. Each day brought new challenges, each one more daunting than the last. The *physical* toll of caring for Willard was immense, but it was the *emotional* strain that weighed heaviest on her heart.

Mary felt a deep sadness as she watched the man she loved most in the world struggle with pain and fear. The lost look in his eyes became a constant reminder of their shared anguish. She battled with feelings of helplessness, unable to shield Willard from the relentless progression of his illness.

She often found herself sitting alone in their bedroom, staring at the photographs that lined the dresser. Pictures of happier times - family vacations, anniversaries, the birth of their children. Each image a sharp contrast to the present reality. The sight of other women with their healthy husbands stirred a mix of emotions within her. A sense of unfairness along with growing anger of the seemingly cruel circumstances ate at her thoughts.

Mary's faith, which had been her bedrock for so long, faced its own trial. She struggled to reconcile her belief in a loving, all-powerful God with the suffering that Willard was enduring. In her darkest moments, she found herself questioning everything she had held dear. Yet, despite her doubts, she clung to the enduring love she and Willard shared, finding comfort in their unbreakable bond. But as Willard's condition worsened, Mary prepared herself for the inevitable.

The thought of life without him was almost unbearable, but she knew she had to be strong.

When Willard finally transitioned and passed away, Mary felt an overwhelming sense of loss, a void that no amount of time could ever truly fill.

In the months that followed, Mary faced the daunting task of rebuilding her life. The grief was a constant companion, but so were the memories of a love that had stood the test of time. As she navigated the uncertain terrain of widowhood, she drew strength from the lessons learned during their 45 years together.

## My Dearest

I can only imagine the depth of emotions you're facing as you deal with your husband's illness. These moments can feel heavy and uncertain, and I want you to know - your feelings are valid. Your pain is real, and it deserves to be acknowledged.

Talking with your husband about his condition can stir emotions you wish you didn't have to feel, but those conversations are necessary. Sharing your fears, hopes, and thoughts with him helps keep your connection strong. Your openness is not a sign of weakness - it's proof of how deeply you love him.

Making practical decisions about his health and end-of-life care can be overwhelming. It's okay to feel lost or unsure. These discussions may drain you emotionally, but they also bring clarity and preparation. Rely on your support system - family, friends, and caregivers. Allow them to help carry the weight. Take care of yourself too. Get rest, talk to someone, and do the things that still bring you peace. Self-care isn't selfish - it's how you stay strong for him.

As your roles and responsibilities shift, the change can feel like walking an emotional tightrope. But talking openly with your husband about these changes can ease that strain. Your ability to adapt shows your resilience and faith in this difficult season.

Grief will walk beside you through this journey. Give yourself permission to feel it. Don't hide from your sadness or guilt - face them head-on. Support groups and counseling can help you process your emotions and remind you that you're not alone. Hearing others share their pain can help you see your own heart more clearly.

Even through all of this, look for moments of joy and connection. Treasure the memories you've already made, and create new ones while you still can. Whether it's quiet time together or doing something small that makes you both smile, these moments matter more than ever.

Please remember - you are not alone in this. Your strength, your love, and your presence are what he needs most right now. The calmer and more at peace you are, the more comfort he'll feel in his final days.

Through your patience and compassion, you're giving him something far greater than medicine - peace of mind.

## **LIFE AFTER DEATH FOR HER**

Losing the man you love to illness can feel like your entire world has been flipped upside down. The first few months - sometimes even years - can feel unreal, like you're walking through a dream you can't wake up from. Everything that once made sense suddenly feels distant, and the pain can be unbearable.

Soon after, you might feel lost, angry, or numb. The routines you once shared - the morning conversations, the inside jokes, even the quiet moments - are gone. That emptiness can echo louder than any noise.

With time, grief becomes a puzzle that you slowly start piecing together. Some days you'll feel strong and capable, and others you'll break down over something small - a song, a smell, or an old photograph. Healing isn't linear. It's messy, unpredictable, and deeply personal. You begin to rediscover who you are outside of the relationship, which can be both painful and freeing. Talking with friends, leaning on family, or seeking therapy can help you find your footing again. Healing takes effort, but every small step forward counts. Over time, the sharp sting of pain softens into something gentler. The memories that once broke you will one day bring you peace. You'll smile when you think of his laughter instead of crying for what's gone.

Eventually, you start meeting new parts of yourself - parts that survived, adapted, and grew stronger. You'll find comfort in small things again: hobbies, laughter, prayer, travel, or simply sitting in silence without the weight of constant grief. You'll realize that life hasn't erased him; it's simply finding a way to carry him with you.

Support from others makes all the difference. Sharing stories, crying, and even laughing with people who understand helps you release the weight little by little. Over time, you may find new purpose - living in a way that honors the love you shared.

The pain never completely disappears, but it changes. It becomes a part of who you are, a reminder that you once loved deeply and were loved in return. That love becomes your strength, helping you build a new kind of peace.

## Six Activities to Consider After the Loss of a Life Partner

1. Support Groups - Joining a group of others who've lost someone can bring a sense of belonging. Sharing your story and hearing theirs reminds you that grief is universal, and you're not alone. If you can't find one nearby, online groups can provide the same comfort.

2. Hobbies and Creative Outlets - Expressing yourself through art, writing, music, gardening, or any creative outlet gives your emotions a voice. Even trying something new can help you reconnect with joy.

3. Volunteer Work - Helping others often brings unexpected healing. Giving your time to someone in need allows your pain to serve a purpose and helps fill the emptiness with compassion.

4. Educational Pursuits - Taking a class or learning a new skill can help you grow beyond your grief. Education gives you something new to focus on and introduces you to people who share your interests.

5. Traveling - Seeing new places doesn't mean you're running from pain - it means you're reminding yourself that life still exists beyond it. Traveling opens your mind to new experiences and helps you create fresh memories alongside the old ones.

6. Fitness and Wellness Activities - Taking care of your body helps your mind heal. Whether it's yoga, walking, or joining a fitness class, physical movement releases stress and connects you with others on their own journeys of recovery.

Every step you take, no matter how small, is proof that you're still moving forward. You're not forgetting him - you're honoring him by continuing to live.

## How Does He Feel

When a man faces the reality of his own death, his emotions run deep. There's fear, sadness, and reflection - but most of all, there's love. His first thought is often about you. He worries about how you'll handle life without him. Will you be okay? Will you have enough support? Your strength gives him peace. When he sees you remain calm and steady, it helps him rest easier, knowing you'll find your way even when he's gone.

He also struggles with thoughts of another man stepping into the life he built with you. The idea of someone else walking through his home, sitting where he sat, or holding you the way he did can cut deeply. It's not always jealousy - it's more about the feeling of being replaced in the story he still wants to be part of. Deep down, though, if he truly loves you, what he wants most is for you to be happy, even if that happiness comes after he's gone.

He'll think about the mark he left on the world - his legacy. Did he live right? Did he do enough for his family? Did he teach his children what they need to know? These questions often circle in his mind. He wants to know that his presence mattered, that he'll be remembered as a good man, a good husband, and a good father. That's where you can bring him peace - by reminding him of the impact he's already made and the love he's already given.

He'll grieve the milestones he won't get to see: his child's graduation, their wedding day, or even simple family moments like Sunday dinners or watching movies together. The realization that he won't be there for those moments can hurt more than the illness itself.

If he's spiritual, he may wrestle with the unknown of what comes next. The thought of death can bring both fear and comfort. Faith can help him make peace with the idea that his body may leave, but his soul continues. It helps him believe that love doesn't end - it just changes form.

In his final days, his focus shifts from fear to peace. He starts to cherish time more - each conversation, each touch, each shared silence. He'll begin putting things in order - insurance, wills, last words - because he doesn't want you to carry those burdens alone. These are his final acts of love.

Every dying man faces a mix of emotions - love, regret, fear, and gratitude. But what remains constant is his desire for the people he loves to be okay. That's what gives him peace in the end.

**Six Ways to Bring Him Peace in His Final Days**

1. Spend Quality Time Together - Sit with him. Talk, laugh, hold his hand. The memories you make now will comfort you later and remind him he's not alone.

2. Express Love Often - Tell him what he means to you. Remind him of the good he's done and the impact he's made. Those words can ease his spirit.

3. Create Comfort - Make his space peaceful and pain-free. Soft music, favorite meals, or old photos can help him feel at ease.

4. Help Fulfill His Wishes - Whether it's a final trip, a letter to write, or a promise to keep, help him complete what he needs to feel at peace.

5. Offer Spiritual Support - If faith matters to him, pray together or invite someone he trusts spiritually. If not, simple conversations about what he believes can bring calm.

6. Build His Legacy - Encourage him to record messages, write letters, or leave advice for his loved ones. These lasting gifts give him purpose in his final moments.

Every man wants to know he mattered. Helping him feel that truth before he leaves this world gives his final days meaning and peace.

## LIFE'S LAST STOP

When life starts to slow down and the end feels near, most people don't fear death itself - they fear being forgotten. They want to know their time here meant something. As the final chapters are written, what matters most isn't money or status; it's the love we gave and the people we touched.

There's an old saying: *"A tree is known by its fruit."* The fruits of our lives are our actions, our kindness, and the memories we leave behind. Every hug, every lesson, every act of love becomes part of our legacy.

When we look back, we realize that life was never really about what we owned or what titles we held. It was about who we shared it with. It's the laughter in the kitchen, the long talks at night, and the quiet moments of peace beside someone we love that define who we are.

As death approaches, we begin to see that success isn't measured by achievements but by impact. Did we make someone's day better? Did we love deeply? Did we forgive easily? These questions matter more than any bank account ever will.

At the core of it, everyone wants the same thing - to know they mattered. To know that someone will smile when they hear their name. That's where peace comes from. Knowing that the love you gave out into the world will echo long after you're gone.

Our stories don't end when our hearts stop beating. They continue through the people we've loved. Each person we touched carries a piece of us forward. That's how we live forever - not in fame or fortune, but in memory and love.

So as you near life's last stop, remember this: your true legacy is written in hearts, not in history books. What you built in love will outlive you. The people you poured into will carry your name, your lessons, and your spirit.

Because in the end, your *forever* isn't measured in days… it's measured in the lives you've touched.

# Your Voice Matters

Thank you for taking this journey with me. If this book touched you in any way, please consider leaving a review on Amazon. Your words have the power to inspire someone else to find the clarity they need.

SCAN W/YOUR PHONE CAMERA TO ORDER

# KNOW THY MAN
## S<small>TANDARD</small> E<small>DITION</small>

T<small>HE</small> 4 S<small>TAGES OF A</small> C<small>HEATING</small> M<small>AN</small>

### **1 Peter 3:8-9 (NLT):**

Finally, all of you should be of one mind. Sympathize with each other. Love each other as brothers and sisters. Be tenderhearted, and keep a humble attitude. Don't repay evil for evil. Don't retaliate with insults when people insult you. Instead, pay them back with a blessing. That is what God has called you to do, and he will grant you his blessing.

May Christ bless you on your new journey!

www.ingramcontent.com/pod-product-compliance
Lightning Source LLC
Chambersburg PA
CBHW022001160426
43197CB00007B/221